Amber Pike

EXPLORING THE BIBLE THROUGH HISTORY

HENDRICKSON PUBLISHERS

ROSE KIDZ

Exploring the Bible through History

RoseKidz® is an imprint of
Rose Publishing, LLC
P.O. Box 3473
Peabody, Massachusetts 01961-3473 USA
www.hendricksonrose.com\rosekidz

Managing Editor: Karen McGraw
Assistant Editor: Talia Messina
Editorial and Production Associate: Drew McCall
Cover and Interior Design: Drew McCall
Illustrations: Havilah Racette

ISBN: 978-1-62862-785-5
RoseKidz® reorder# R50024
RELIGION/Christian Ministry/Children

Printed in the United States of America
Printed January 2020

Contents

How to Use This Book

Time Line Materials

For each lesson, you will need a time line and time line marker (a sticker or paper arrow to identify your place on the time line). These will collectively be referred to as Time Line Materials throughout this book. We recommend using Rose's *Giant 10-Foot Bible Time Line* (found at www.hendricksonrose.com), or you can make your own time line with the reproducible coloring pages (see page 5 for more information). We acknowledge that all dates in these chapters are approximate.

Chapter Layout

Each chapter in this teaching resource is divided into six sections:

Introduce It!

Begin every lesson by placing a time line tracker on the time line so kids can see where they are in history. This section emphasizes the context of the lesson in the greater scheme of the Bible as whole. It also includes a lesson overview, a memory verse, and a recap of what happened in the previous chapter.

Tell It!

Tell the Bible story to the children. Depending on their age level, have children look up the Bible references to follow along.

Pray It!

Encourage children to connect with God through prayer. Each lesson offers a sample prayer that connects to the themes of the lesson. Feel free to use it or to make up your own.

Apply It!

Welcome to the activities section! Here you will find five Bible-centric activities that work with both large or small groups. These activities include:

- **Show It:** an object lesson
- **Act It Out:** a reenactment of the Bible lesson
- **Play It:** a game based on the Bible lesson
- **Craft It:** a craft based on the Bible lesson
- **Snack It:** a snack that easily ties to the Bible lesson

Use as many activities as you want. You can even intersperse them between the Tell It! sections to keep the kids' attention.

APPLY IT!

Talk about It!

These life application questions allow kids to process what they've learned from the Bible story. They are divided into two sections:

- **Basic Questions** are appropriate for all age groups.
- **Go Further** questions are more difficult and are better suited for upper elementary children.

Be creative about using these questions:

- Use them in a small group circle.
- Talk about them during the snack or craft activity.
- Ask the winners of the games to answer them for bonus points.

The possibilities are endless!

Wrap It Up!

End each chapter with a summary of the key points from the Bible lesson.

Reproducible Coloring Pages

At the back of the book, you will notice a coloring page for each chapter. Use these resources to:

- **Build your own time line.** As you go through each chapter, tape the coloring pages together to build a time line. You can make one for the whole class or make a copy for each child, and they can make their own time line from lesson to lesson.
- **Fill class time.** If you find you have extra time in your lesson, hand out the coloring pages to keep the children occupied.
- **Make it a discussion.** Ask the **Talk about It!** questions as children color.
- **Use as take-home resources.** Send the children home with these reproducible coloring pages so they can share what they learn with family members.

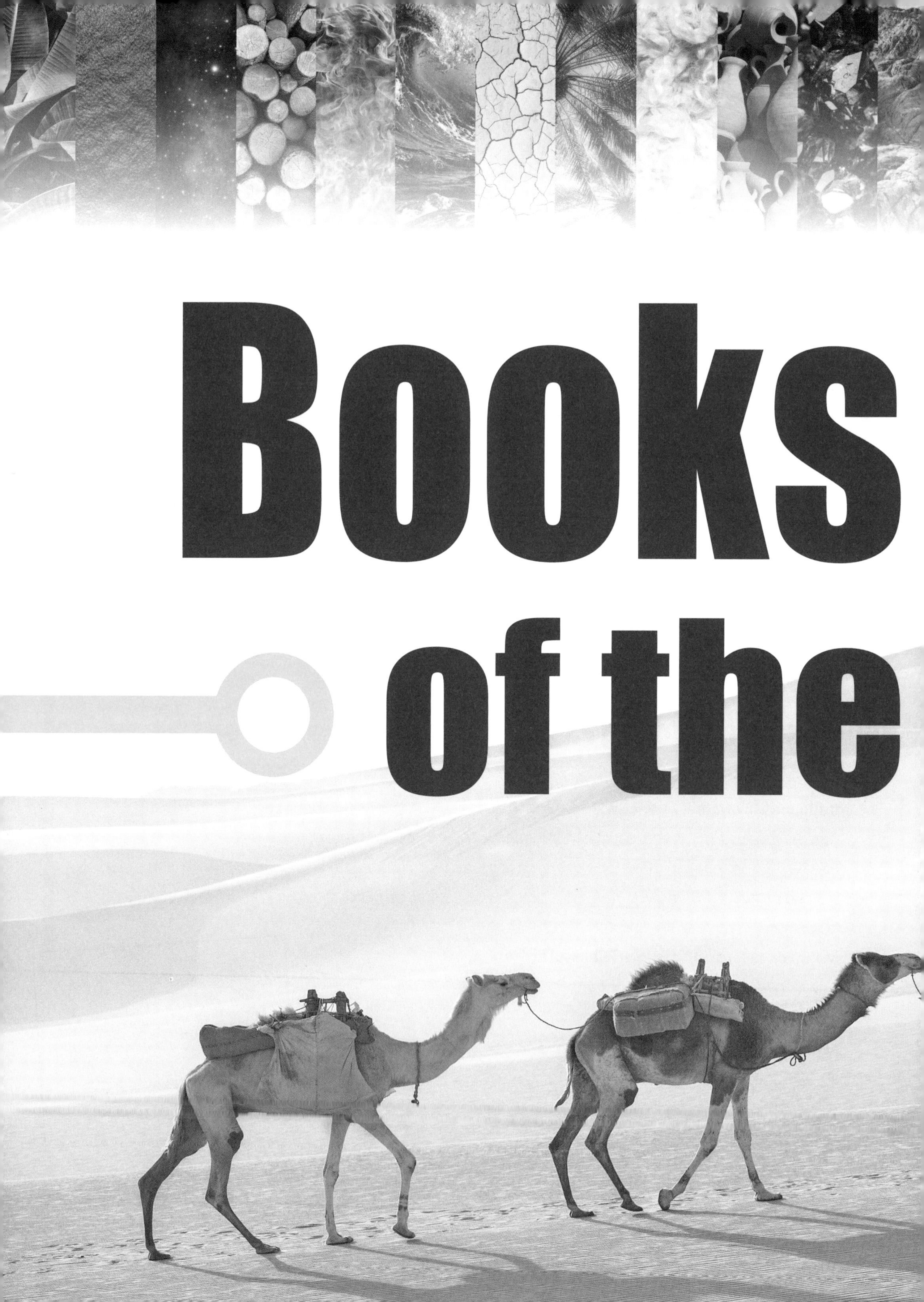
Books
of the

LAW

1
LESSON OVERVIEW
Children will learn about creation,
who was present at creation,
and the result of the Fall.

Genesis 1–3
Adam and Eve

Introduce It!

Time Line

About 4000 B.C.

Key Events & People

Creation, the Fall; Adam, Eve

Memory Verse

In the beginning God created the heavens and the earth.

Genesis 1:1

Time Line Materials needed. (See p. 4.)

Today we are starting our journey through history, and we will begin at the very beginning. "In the beginning God created the heavens and the earth" (Genesis 1:1). Let's pray and thank God for all of the wonderful things he has made. Pause to pray.

To start at the very beginning of time, we need to travel back to the beginning of creation, at about 4000 B.C. Place the time line marker at the beginning of the time line.

Now that we know the WHEN, what about the WHERE? We cannot point out where creation took place on Earth because we don't know! Some people say creation took place somewhere in the Middle East because Genesis talks about the Tigris and Euphrates Rivers (Genesis 1:14), which are still around today. We may not know the exact location, but the Bible does tell us lots of other details about how God made our world!

Tell It!

Choose a way to tell the story while reading the account from the Bible or telling it in your own words. Ideas for creative storytelling include acting it out, using props, or incorporating pictures.

Beginning

In the Bible, where does it talk about the beginning of the world? Hint: think beginning. Children respond. That's right, if we want to read about the beginning of the world, we need to start at Genesis, the beginning of the Bible! Genesis is the very first book of the Old Testament. In fact, its name means beginning.

GENESIS

Read Genesis 1:1–2.

So, what was there in the beginning? Children respond. Nothing! Before God created the heavens and the earth, the earth was empty; there was nothing. This is important, so make sure you remember it.

Creation

As we dive into the creation story, keep these questions in mind:

a. What did God create?
b. How did God create?
c. What did God think of his creation?

The From Nothing object lesson on page 12 pairs well with this section.

FROM NOTHING

Select volunteers to read the following passages. Pause between each day of creation to answer the three questions above.

1. Genesis 1:3–5
    a. *Light*
    a. *He spoke.*
    a. *It was good.*
1. Genesis 1:6–8
    a. *Sky*
    a. *He spoke.*
    a. *It doesn't say.*
1. Genesis 1:9–13
    a. *Land, seas, and plants*
    a. *He spoke.*
    a. *It was good.*
1. Genesis 1:14–19
    a. *A light for the day (sun), a light for the night (moon), and stars*
    b. *He spoke.*
    c. *It was good.*
1. Genesis 1:20–23
    a. *Sea creatures and birds*
    b. *He spoke.*
    c. *It was good.*
1. Genesis 1:24–31
    a. *Animals and humans*
    b. *He spoke.*
    c. *It was very good.*

God spoke everything into existence from nothing.

The Fall of Man

Adam was the first man ever created. Even though he was surrounded by beautiful plants and animals, he was lonely. He wanted a friend. So God created Eve, and God put them in charge of all of the plants and animals.

Adam and Eve lived in the Garden of Eden, and God told them that they could eat from any tree except one. The Tree of the Knowledge of Good and Evil was off limits. This specific tree wasn't for them, so they weren't supposed to eat it. Are there any foods that you aren't allowed to eat because they'll make you sick? Children respond.

One day, Eve was wandering in the garden alone when Satan, God's enemy, appeared to her. He was disguised as a snake, and he had some questions for Eve.

Read Genesis 3:1–24.

Satan tempted Adam and Eve on that day. Adam and Eve questioned God's word. They chose to disobey God and eat the fruit. At that moment, sin entered the world, and God's perfect creation was no longer perfect.

Pray It!

Dear God, thank you for creating me and my family. Thank you for all the wonderful things in the world that you gave us to take care of. Please help me to take care of my things, too. In Jesus' name, amen.

Apply It!

Choose any of these activities for your lesson. Use more than one if time allows. For any of these activities, discuss the **Talk about It!** questions on page 17 as time allows.

Show It!

From Nothing

Materials
1 small cup of alphabet shaped objects (cereal, crackers, beads, etc.) for each child

Overview

Kids try to spell their name by dumping out a cup of letters. Illustrates that we cannot create something from nothing.

We cannot create something from nothing. If I want to grow tomatoes, I need tomato seeds. If I want to make a sandwich, I need bread and sandwich toppings. We are going to do a simple experiment to show us how only our all-powerful God could have created our world from nothing.

Directions

1. Give each child a cup of alphabet shapes. Their goal is to dump out their cups and have the letters land randomly, spelling their name.
2. Cups must be emptied in one motion, not letter by letter.
3. Children can collect their alphabet shapes and try again as time allows.

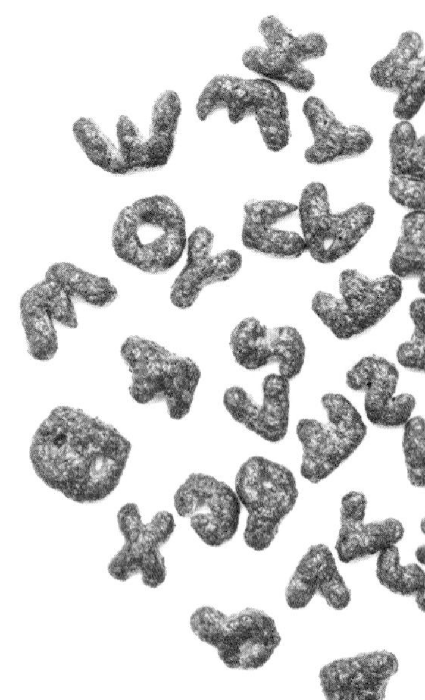

Conversation

Could anyone spell their name? Children respond. **No! We had letters and could not make our names appear. We didn't even start from nothing like God did at creation.**

Our world wasn't created by random chance or accident. An intelligent, all-powerful Creator made the world and all that is in it because of his great love for us!

The Fall of Man

Overview

Children vote on what they think is good or bad. Reinforces that God thought what he created was good.

After each day of creation, what did God say about his creation? Children respond. **"It was good." Let's play a little game to see what God would think is good or not.**

Directions

Instruct children to stand up if the item you read would be considered good and to sit down if it is not considered good.

- Sunshine
- Fruit
- Sin
- Beaches
- Sickness
- Snow
- Friendship
- Death
- Stars

Conversation

All of the things that were not good have something in common. Can anyone think of what it is? Children respond. The things in our world that are not good are all a result of sin entering the world.

When God created the world, everything he made was good! The world was perfect—no sickness, no death, nothing bad. Then, Adam and Eve made a choice. We do not know how long after creation this took place, but Genesis 3 tells us exactly what happened that forever changed God's perfect creation.

Act It Out!

It Was Good

Overview

Children are assigned a day of creation and act it out when called upon.

Directions

1. Assign each child a day of creation. There can be more than one child per day. If your class is too large for all children to have a chance to participate, assign children into groups that will act out a day together.
2. Summarize the biblical account of creation. As you do, the children will stand up and silently act out something that God made on their assigned days. For example, a child assigned to day three could pretend to be a tree.

Conversation

Each day, after God was finished creating, he said it was good. Everything God created, from the oceans to the trees, from the stars to the bees, was all good! God created a perfect, sinless world for us to live in!

Play It!

Creation Day Countdown

Materials

a soft ball or another small object for children to grab

masking tape

Overview

Children are assigned as creations of either day five or six and must race to steal a ball from the other team. Helps kids memorize the creation days.

Preparation

Put down a line of tape in the middle of the room.

Directions

1. Divide children into two teams, one on each side of a tape line. Teams will face each other on opposite sides of the line in the middle.
2. Place the ball in the middle of the tape line.
3. Assign each child on team one as either bird or man. Assign each child on team two as either fish or animal.
4. When the leader calls out "day five" or "day six," the children who have been created on that day will race to collect the ball from the middle without getting tagged by the other team. Note that on day five the fish and the birds will play and on day 6 the men or the animals will play.
5. If the child with the ball can make it back to their line without getting tagged, their team answers a **Talk about It!** question from page 17.

Optional

Depending on your class size, multiple groups or more specific animal names (within the four categories) may be needed.

Conversation

Great job remembering what God created on days five and six! Who remembers, out of all of the things God created on day five and day six, what was the most important creation? Children respond. **Humankind is God's most special creation!**

Craft It!

New Animal Creations

Overview

Children draw a brand-new animal.

> **Materials**
>
> paper
>
> colored pencils or markers
>
> **Optional:** pictures of amazing and unique creations (nature scenes, platypus, blob fish, space/stars, etc.)

Conversation

God made some amazing creations: colorful flowers, crazy animals like the platypus and the blob fish, and outer space. Out of all that he made, which do you think is his favorite, most prized creation? Children respond.

His most prized creation is us! Unlike anything else God made, humans are made "in the image of God." We are made with the ability to talk and create. Most importantly, we are created with the ability to choose to follow Christ. We can receive forgiveness for our sins by choosing to follow God. God's Word tells us that we are even more important than the angels!

To practice being creative, you are going to try to create your own animal! Since we don't have God's power, we can't create from nothing, like he did.

Directions

Hand out paper and colored pencils or markers.

Keep these things in mind while you create:

- Where will your animal live?
- How will it eat?
- Can it protect itself?
- What will it look like?
- What will you name it?

Snack It!

It Was Good Snack Mix

Materials

resealable plastic snack bags (1 per child)

snack mix ingredients (such as cereal, pretzels, dried fruit, candy, crackers, marshmallows, etc.)

bowls for each ingredient

Overview

Children create their own snack mix.

Preparation

Put snack ingredients in separate bowls.

Directions

Children pick the ingredients to create their own unique, colorful snack mix by selecting ingredients from the bowls, and placing them in their snack bags. Children seal uneaten snacks in the bag to take home.

Conversation

God created a colorful and wonderful world for us to live in. God said everything he made was good.

1. Did you fill your snack bags with lots of colorful, good snacks? Which snacks are your favorite?
2. What kinds of good snacks do you think God made for Adam and Eve to enjoy in the garden?
3. If you could make your own garden, what kind of food would grow on the trees?

Talk about It!

Basic Questions

1. Who was present at creation? *God, Jesus, and the Holy Spirit*.
2. How did God create the world? *By speaking it into existence.*
3. On what day did God create the sun? *Day 4.*
4. On what day did God create birds? *Day 5.*
5. What did God think about everything he created? *It was good.*
6. What was the name of the garden that God created for Adam and Eve? *The Garden of Eden.*
7. Who tempted Adam and Eve in the garden? *The serpent/Satan.*
8. How did Adam and Eve sin? *They disobeyed God by eating the fruit that was off-limits.*

Go Further

1. Name one of the punishments Adam and Eve received for their sin. See Genesis 3:16–19. *Kicked out of the Garden of Eden, had to work at growing food, pain in childbirth, the serpent will bruise his heel, daily hard work.*
2. How do we know we can trust that the Bible tells the true account of creation?
   - Who wrote the Bible? (See 2 Timothy 3:16–17.) *Many different people across many generations physically wrote the Bible, but it was inspired by God.*
   - Can God lie? (See Numbers 23:19.) *No.*
   - If God wrote the Bible, and God cannot lie, what does that tell us about the Bible's account of creation? *It is truth.*

Wrap It Up!

Refer to the time line. About 6,000 years ago, God created our amazing world. The plants, the animals, even the sun and moon and stars, were all created for us. Out of all of these amazing things that God created, his most important creation was humankind. We are made in the image of God and made with the choice to follow God. We have the chance to live forever with God if we choose to follow him, all because of his great love for us!

2

LESSON OVERVIEW

Through the account of Noah and the flood, children will see that God saved humanity with the ark, and one day God will once again save humanity—through his Son.

Genesis 6–9

Noah and the Flood

Introduce It!

Time Line
2344 B.C.

Key Events & People
The Flood; Noah

Memory Verse
I am the way, the truth, and the life. No one can come to the Father except through me.
John 14:6

Time Line Materials needed. (See p. 4.)

Begin the lesson in prayer. Thank God for the gift of Jesus and the salvation he offers.

After Adam and Eve left the Garden of Eden, their family grew and grew. As the number of people in the world grew, so did their sin and wickedness. The Bible tells us that the people living on Earth were so wicked that every thought in their hearts was evil. There was, however, one righteous man. His name was Noah.

God told Noah that he was going to destroy the earth and everything in it with a worldwide flood. Noah was told exactly how to build the ark that would keep him, his family, and the animals safe. Around 2344 B.C., (Place time line marker at 2344 B.C.) Noah was 600 years old, and God's judgment began with a worldwide flood.

Tell It!

Choose a way to tell the story while reading the account from the Bible or telling it in your own words. Ideas for creative storytelling include acting it out, using props, or incorporating pictures.

Noah Obeyed God

The ark had to survive the flood waters and keep Noah's family and all the animals safe. We don't know what Noah did for work, or if he even knew how to build a boat. We *do* know that God told Noah exactly how to build the ark, though! Let's read God's Word to see what God told Noah to do.

Read Genesis 6:14–22.

How did God say the ark was to be built? Children respond.

The ark was to be:

- 450 feet long
- 75 feet wide
- 45 feet tall
- 3 decks
- One door
- Cypress/gopher wood
- Coated in pitch

Does this sound like a large boat or a small boat? Children respond. This was a huge boat. It was longer than one and a half football fields! It had to be big enough to survive a worldwide flood, plus hold two of each kind of animal.

What Does "Animal Kind" Mean?

Noah was to take two of each kind of animal with him on the ark. Does that mean he needed to take two of each breed of dog on the ark? Children respond. No! There are several hundred different breeds of dogs. There are Dalmatians, shepherds, poodles, Chihuahuas, and the list goes on and on. Though there are lots of different breeds of dogs, there is just one dog kind or family.

How many of the dog family would Noah need on the ark then? Children respond. Two! Noah did need a big boat to fit all the animals inside, but he only needed two of each kind. The ark would have had plenty of room for all of the animals and more!

A Worldwide Flood

Let's make it sound like a rainstorm. We will start by patting our legs softly. Then, as the storm grows, we will pat louder and louder. Keep it up while I read from Genesis, but when I read about the rain stopping, I want you to stop our rainstorm sound.

Read Genesis 7:11–12, 17–19, 8:1–4.

God's Word tells us that Noah's family was safe inside the ark. What happened to all of the other people in the world? Children respond. Remember, the flood was God's judgment and punishment on the world. The people had become so wicked, so full of sin, that God destroyed the world and everyone in it.

Does anyone know how God feels about sin? Children respond. He hates sin! Romans 6:23 tells us, "The wages of sin is death." The punishment for sin is death. The people of Noah's time were punished for their sins through the flood. Because Noah was righteous and followed God, his family was saved from the flood.

Today, we are still punished for our sins. Instead of being punished with a worldwide flood, our punishment today is separation from God. Just as there was only one way for Noah and his family to be saved (through the ark), there is one way for us to be saved through Jesus.

Pray It!

Dear God, thank you for protecting me when I get into trouble. Help me to follow your rules and be good to all people, even if they are not nice to me. In Jesus' name, amen.

Apply It!

Choose any of these activities for your lesson. Use more than one if time allows. For any of these activities, discuss the **Talk about It!** questions on page 25 as time allows.

Show It!

An Important Job

Take your index card and cut it so your WHOLE body can fit through the card. Give children several minutes to attempt the task.

It's hard to do this job without being told how to do it, wasn't it? Do you think it can be done? Let's see.

Materials
index cards (1 per child, plus extras)
scissors

Overview

Children are given a seemingly impossible task just like Noah was given.

Directions

1. Fold the card in half-length wise the "hot-dog" way.
2. Make a cut, starting at the folded edge and ending just before the open edge. Make another cut starting from the open edge and ending just before the folded edge. Continue cutting the rest of the index card by alternating back and forth between starting points. Be careful not to cut all the way through! The narrower your cuts are, the wider your end result will be.
3. Open the card. Leave the top and bottom edge intact.
4. Cut down the middle.
5. Gently stretch out the card.
6. Step into the circle it makes.

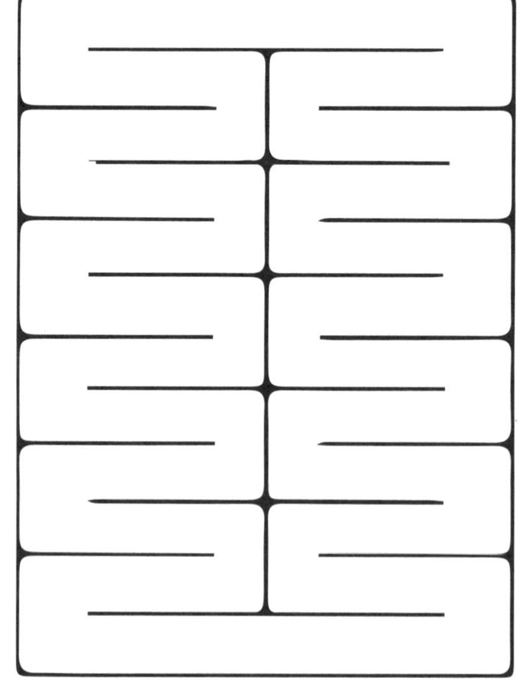

Conversation

It wasn't an impossible task! But it would have been a lot easier if I had told you exactly how to do it, wouldn't it? Noah had a big, important task. God told him to build an ark big enough to hold himself, his family, and two of each animal kind. Thankfully, God told Noah exactly how to build it!

Act It Out!

Two by Two

Overview

Children will act out when God sent the animals to the ark, two by two, by finding their matching pair.

Directions

1. Pass out animal card pictures or names to the children.
2. Children must act like their animal searching for their match.
3. Once children find their match, they can have a seat.

Materials

cards or pictures of matching animals (1 per child). Cards should include pairs of animal kinds such as bears, tigers, dogs, etc.

Conversation

Genesis tells us that God sent the animals in pairs to Noah and the ark. The floodwaters came for forty days and forty nights, but God kept Noah, his family, and all of the animals safe on the ark.

Play It!

Feed the Animals

Overview

The goal is to collect food for imaginary animals by filling baskets.

Materials

paper wads or small balls (50–100)

2–4 baskets or buckets

Directions

1. Divide children into two to four teams, depending on your group size. If you have an odd number of children, have a few of them be the animals. They can cheer on their team with animal sounds.
2. Give each team a basket at opposite ends of the playing area. If you are playing with four teams, put them in the corners of the room.
3. Place the paper wads or balls in the middle. Tell the children the wads are animal food.
4. Teams race to collect "food" and run back to their basket to feed their imaginary animals. Children can only get one piece of food at a time.
5. The team with the most "food" in their basket gets to answer a **Talk about It!** question from page 25.
6. For an extra challenge, allow children to steal food from the opposing team's baskets.

Conversation

You all worked super hard collecting food to feed your imaginary animals! Have you ever stopped to think about all the hard work Noah and his family did to care for the animals on the ark? If time allows, talk about what it might have been like to care for the animals on the ark for a year.

Craft It!

Rainbow Rocks

Materials

rocks (1 per child)

acrylic paint (red, orange, yellow, green, blue, purple)

paintbrushes (1 per child)

Overview

Children will paint their rocks with rainbows or rainbow colors to remind them of God's promise to Noah, and God's promise to us.

Conversation

What did God put the rainbow in the sky to remind Noah of? Children respond. That's right. The rainbow reminds us of God's promise to never again flood the whole world. God kept Noah and his family safe in the ark. God promises to save us, too. Our rainbow rocks can remind us that God's Word tells us that anyone who believes in Jesus will be saved!

Snack It!

Ocean Wave Delight

Materials

blue jello cups (1 per child)

whipped cream

spoons

Overview

Children eat a snack that looks like water.

Directions

Top jello with whipped cream and give to children with a spoon to eat.

Conversation

Who remembers how long the flood lasted? Children respond. That's right, it rained for 40 days and 40 nights. Does that mean after 40 days there was no more water? Children respond. No, the flood waters had to go down. The water covered the whole earth for about a year!

Talk about It!

Basic Questions

1. What did the rainbow God put in the sky mean? (See Genesis 9:11–17.) *Symbolized God's promise to never flood the earth again.*
2. Why was God sending the flood on earth? *The people were full of wickedness.*
3. What one man was righteous? *Noah.*
4. God told Noah to do what? *To build an ark.*
5. Who went inside the ark? *Noah, his wife, his three sons, and their wives. Also, two of every kind of animal.*
6. How long did it rain? *40 days and 40 nights.*

Go Further

1. How can we be saved from the punishment of sin? (See John 3:16, John 14:6, Romans 10:9.) *By believing in Jesus.*
2. What promises does God make to us? (See John 14:6, Deuteronomy 31:6.) *Jesus is the only way to salvation. He will never abandon us.*

Wrap It Up!

Refer to the time line. The flood was a scary time for unbelievers, but Noah's faith in God saved his family and the animals. And God promised that he would never again flood the whole earth. Because of Noah's obedience to God about 4000 years ago, humanity was saved from God's punishment. Only through Christ Jesus can we be saved from our sins, forgiven, and given eternal life with God the Father.

3

LESSON OVERVIEW

Through God's covenant with Abram, children will see how God cares for his people.

Genesis 12–15

Abram is Called

Introduce It!

Time Line
2166 B.C.

Key Events & People
God makes a covenant with Abram; Abram, Sarai

Memory Verse
I will bless those who bless you and curse those who treat you with contempt. All the families on earth will be blessed through you.
Genesis 12:3

Time Line Materials needed. (See p. 4.)

Begin the lesson in prayer. Thank God for caring for his children and praise him for his sovereignty.

Our last lesson was about Noah and the flood. Refer to the time line, 2344 B.C. Because of their faithfulness to God, Noah and his family were the only humans who survived the flood. They would tell the story of how God saved them for many generations.

Several generations after Noah, there was a faithful man named Abram. God was pleased with Abram's faith and he wanted to bless him. God spoke to Abram about big plans for his people. At that time (place time line marker on 2166 B.C.), Abram was living in a place called Haran.

Tell It!

Choose a way to tell the story while reading the account from the Bible or telling it in your own words. Ideas for creative storytelling include acting it out, using props, or incorporating pictures.

God Calls Abram

Read Genesis 12:1–5.

God told Abram to leave his country, the people he knew, and even his family. God was going to show Abram the land that he prepared for him.

What promise did God give Abram when he told him to move? Children respond. God promised Abram that he was going to make him into a great nation and bless him.

Did God give him any other clues about how he would bless him or make him into a great nation? Children respond. No! Abram had to trust God and the future he promised.

Abram chose to obey God. When Abram was seventy-five years old, he packed up his possessions, his wife Sarai, his nephew Lot, and all of his possessions, and he headed for the land of Canaan.

Abram and Lot Split

Abram had traveled with all of his possessions and family to Bethel. Abram's nephew, Lot, had brought his family and herds of animals, too. As God began to bless Abram and Lot, they became more and more wealthy. Between the two of them, there were too many servants and animals for the land to sustain.

Read Genesis 13:5–12.

Abram and Lot split up so they would each have enough to support their families. Abram let Lot decide which land he wanted first so there would not be future fights. Lot settled near Sodom, and Abram settled near Hebron. They both lived with enough space for everyone.

God's Covenant with Abram

God had not forgotten his promise to Abram, but Abram was getting discouraged. Abram and his wife, Sarai, were old. Worse than that, they had no children. God promised to make Abram into a great nation, but Abram did not see how that could happen since he had no children. Abram suggested that his servant could be his heir, but God had other plans.

Sometimes, it is easy for us to get discouraged. We want things to happen right away—the way we want it. But God always has a plan. All we need to do is to be patient and wait on him.

Read Genesis 15:4–5.

God told Abram that he would have many children and grandchildren and great-grandchildren. He would have so many that they would be as numerous as the stars in the sky. Who knows how many stars there are in the night sky? In our galaxy? Children respond. There are too many for us to even count! So, what was God telling Abram? Children respond.

God was reassuring Abram that he had not forgotten his promise to bless him and to make him into a great nation. Although Abram did not have any children, he would soon. His children and great grandchildren would be so numerous, much like the stars in the sky, you would not be able to count them!

Pray It!

Dear Lord, thank you for the promise that you will always be with me. Even when I think things are not going my way, I know you have a plan for me, just like you had a plan for Abram. In Jesus' name, amen.

Apply It!

Choose any of these activities for your lesson. Use more than one if time allows. For any of these activities, discuss the **Talk about It!** questions on page 33 as time allows.

Show It!

Materials

travel games (travel-size board games, magnetic checker and chess set, etc.)

Games on the Go

Overview

Children discuss travel games and songs to discover that God will care for them wherever they go.

God commanded Abram to move his family. It couldn't have been easy for Abram to uproot his family and home, but he did. Abram trusted that God would care for him and his family wherever they went. Let's talk about some things we often do when we travel and discover that God cares for us when we travel and even when we don't!

Directions

Show the travel games you brought with you.

1. Ask the following questions:
    - When might you play a game like this? Children respond.
    - What games do you play on trips with your family? Children respond.
    - Do you have any family-favorite songs that you sing? Children respond.
2. If time allows, play games or sing songs suggested.

Conversation

Wherever we go, God will care for us, just like he cared for Abram and his family.

Act It Out!

Travel Charades

Overview

Children think of a faraway place to go. Class guesses the location through charades.

Today, you are going on a faraway trip, and you will be there for a long time. Long trips require lots of planning. What kind of things do you need to think about before you go? Children respond. Those are great examples! For this game, we are going to focus on these three questions:

1. How will you get there?
2. What will the weather be like when you arrive?
3. What will you do there?

Directions

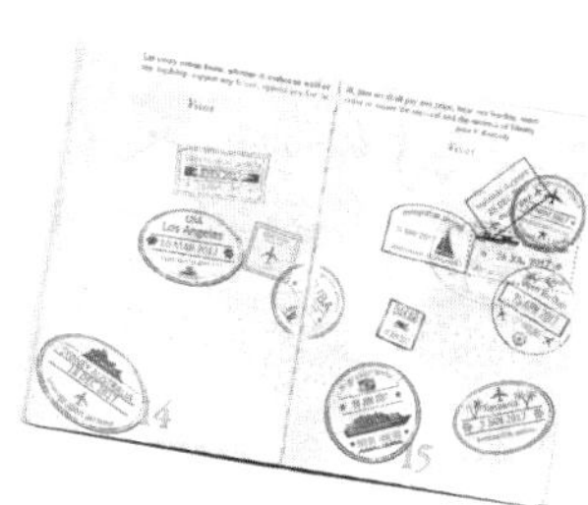

1. Each player thinks of a place they want to go. They must be able to answer the three questions listed above.
2. The first actor stands up and acts out their answer to the first question of "How will I get there?" Children guess car or plane or whatever the transportation is.
3. When the right answer is guessed, the actor acts out the second question. Children guess again.
4. Actor acts out answer to the third question. Children guess the action and the actor's destination. The actor can change actions if the children have a hard time guessing. For example, if the actor is going to Hawaii, they might pretend like they are swimming, but there are many places to where you can swim. So the actor might wave their arms like a Hawaiian dancer.
5. The first person to guess the location gets to be the next actor and answers, or chooses a volunteer to answer, a **Talk about It!** question from page 33.

Optional

If you have a large class, group them into threes. Each group will secretly decide where they are going. Then each person acts out one part of the charade.

Conversation

Great job acting out all those places. You clearly knew a lot about where you were going. When God told Abram to move, Abram did not know anything about the new place. Raise your hand if you've ever moved to a new place. Children respond. Sometimes families move because of a job or maybe to get closer to family. Abram was moving for a different reason. He trusted in God's promise.

Play It!

Materials
masking tape
music

Race to the Music

Overview

Children play a stop-and-go game to reinforce Abram's immediate reaction to move to Canaan.

Directions

1. Use masking tape to make start and finish lines. Children will line up behind the start line.
2. When the music plays, children will walk as fast as they can toward the finish line. When the music stops, they must freeze.
3. If a leader catches racers moving after the music stops, they must go back to the start line.
4. The first child to reach the finish line answers, or chooses a volunteer to answer, a **Talk about It!** question from page 33.

Conversation

You moved super fast in our game! When God told Abram to move to a new land, do you think he wanted to get there in a hurry? Children respond. Whether his trip was fast or not so fast, we do know that Abram obeyed God. God had a plan for Abram's life, just like he has a plan for our lives today.

Craft It!

Stars in the Sky

Overview

Children decorate a memory verse page with stars.

Conversation

What promises did God make to Abram? Children respond. God promised to bless him and said he would have more descendants than there are stars in the sky. To remind us of God's promise to Abram, we are going to create a starry sky with today's memory verse on it.

Materials

- cardstock with memory verse printed on it (1 per child)
- permanent markers
- 1-inch squares of colored tissue paper
- paintbrushes (1 per child)
- cups of water

Directions

1. Draw stars all over the memory verse page. No drawing can be done later, it must be done before the tissue paper is added.
2. Place colored tissue squares over the paper, "painting" them on with water.
3. After the water dries, the tissue paper will peel off, leaving a beautiful color residue.
4. As time allows, answer **Talk about It!** questions found on page 33.

Snack It!

Sand Pudding

Overview

Children eat a snack that resembles desert sand.

Materials

- pudding cup and spoon (1 per child)
- graham crackers, crushed
- spoons

Directions

Top each pudding cup with crushed graham crackers and give to children with a spoon to eat.

Conversation

Our sand pudding snack reminds us of the desert trip that Abram took to Canaan. God told Abram to leave his home and go to the land God promised him. Abram was obedient to God. He packed up his family and possessions and started moving!

Talk about It!

Basic Questions

1. What did God tell Abram to do? *To leave and go to the land he would show him.*
2. Who did Abram take with him? *All his possessions, his wife Sarai, and his nephew Lot and Lot's family.*
3. What promise (or covenant) did God make to Abram? *That he would bless him and make him a great nation.*
4. Why was Abram discouraged with God's promise? *Because he had no children.*
5. How did God remind Abram of his promise? *He told Abram that he would have as many children as there were stars in the sky.*
6. Why did Abram and Lot have to separate? *There were not enough resources in one spot to support both of their families.*
7. Where did Lot choose to live? *Sodom.*
8. Where did Abram live? *Hebron.*
9. What did Abram do to thank God? *Built an altar to the Lord.*

Go Further

1. Did God forget about Abram? Why do you think it took God so long to bless Abram with a child?
2. Does God ever forget about us? What should we do if we feel God has forgotten us?

Wrap It Up!

Refer to the time line. God told Abram that he would bless him and make him into a great nation. As Abram continued to remain childless in his old age, he felt that God had forgotten his promise to him. God did not forget about Abram. He had a plan for Abram's life.

God is always in control and caring for his children! Just like God had a plan for Abram's life, he has a plan for our lives too!

4
LESSON OVERVIEW
God fulfills his promise to give Abraham his son Isaac. Abraham's willingness to sacrifice Isaac is an example of true obedience to God.

Genesis 18,21–22

Isaac and Abraham

Introduce It!

Time Line

2066 B.C.

Key Events & People

God tests Abraham; Abraham, Isaac, Sarah

Time Line Materials needed. (See p. 4.)

Begin the lesson in prayer. Ask God to help us learn what obedience to him looks like and for us to become more obedient to him.

Who remembers Abram? God spoke to Abram and told him it was time to move to the land that God would send him. We know that land was the Promised Land, which God had chosen for his special children, the Israelites. God also made a covenant, a big promise, with Abram that he would make Abram into a great nation.

God changed Abram's name to *Abraham*, which means father of many nations. And he changed Sarai's name to Sarah, promising that she would have a child. It was a great promise, except for one small detail. Abraham and Sarah were very old. Place the time line marker at 2066 B.C.

Memory Verse

At the name of Jesus every knee should bow, in heaven and on earth and under the earth, and every tongue declare that Jesus Christ is Lord, to the glory of God the Father.

Philippians 2:10–11

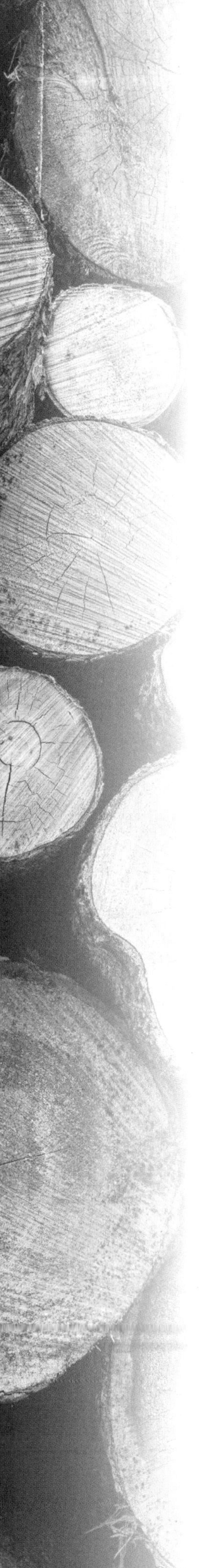

Tell It!

Choose a way to tell the story while reading the account from the Bible or telling it in your own words. Ideas for creative storytelling include acting it out, using props, or incorporating pictures.

The Birth of Isaac

Many years went by, and Abraham and Sarah grew older. Genesis 18 tells us that one day the Lord appeared to Abraham in the form of three visitors. Abraham hurried to make them comfortable and give them food.

As the visitors ate with Abraham, Sarah listened to the conversation. One of the men told Abraham that he would be back around the same time next year, and at that time, Abraham and Sarah would have a son. What do you think Sarah did when she heard that? Children respond. Sarah laughed!

Read Genesis 18:12.

God always keeps his promises, though. Sure enough, a year later, when Abraham was 100 years old, he had a son (refer to the time line). Scripture tells us that, "The LORD kept his word and did for Sarah exactly what he had promised" (Genesis 21:1). Abraham and Sarah were blessed with a baby boy. They named their long-awaited son Isaac. In Hebrew, the name Isaac means he laughs. Sarah thought when other people found out their age, they would laugh, too.

Abraham is Tested

If you had to wait years and years and years for something you wanted before you finally received it, you would love it a lot, right? It might even be your favorite thing in the world, right? Do you think Isaac, the child that Abraham waited and waited for, is what he loved the most?

Read Genesis 22:1–2.

Of course, Abraham loved Isaac, but he loved God more. This was an incredible request! Abraham must have wondered how he'd be able to do what God asked of him. But whatever he might have been thinking, Abraham obeyed.

Early the next morning, he prepared everything he needed—including a knife—got Isaac ready, and the two of them headed off to the place where God told him to go.

Abraham never questioned God's command, even to the point where he picked up his knife in order to sacrifice Isaac. But God called out to stop him. And God provided a sheep caught in a bush for the sacrifice. Abraham didn't have to kill Isaac!

When God tested Abraham, Abraham followed God obediently. He was willing to sacrifice his son Isaac because he trusted what God told him to do. Remember that God had promised to bless Abraham through Isaac's descendants. So even though Abraham did not understand how the promise would be fulfilled, he still obeyed. Abraham trusted God to fulfill his promise to him, no matter what happened.

Pray It!

Dear God, it's really hard to obey when I don't feel like doing something. I just want to do what I want all the time. Help me to listen and obey when other people need me. In Jesus' name, amen.

Apply It!

Choose any of these activities for your lesson. Use more than one if time allows. For any of these activities, discuss the **Talk about It!** questions on page 41 as time allows.

Show It!

Emergency Kit

Materials

large bag with these three items inside: Bible, eraser, a framed photo of a friend and/or family member

Overview

Children explore items that could provide help at times they find it difficult to obey God.

An emergency kit often has bandages, water, and other things you might need in a medical emergency. Today we're going to look at a different kind of emergency kit. It isn't always easy to do what God wants us to do. These are things that can help us in an obedience emergency.

Directions

1. Hold up the bag so that children can see it. Shake the bag so they hear there are objects inside. Invite two or more volunteers to feel the objects from the outside of the bag to see if they can identify what the objects are.
2. After children have guessed what the items are, take them out one at a time and explain how those items can help in an obedience emergency:
   - Bible—the Bible is full of good advice and information about what God wants us to do. Reading Bible stories and verses, especially those about God's love, can encourage us to obey God.
   - Eraser—Erasers are something we use when we make mistakes. When we do something wrong, we can ask God for forgiveness, and it's like he erases the sin away.
   - Framed photo—God gives us people to encourage us to obey him. Our friends and family love and pray for us. That will help us be obedient to God.

Conversation

God wants us to obey him because he knows the very best way for us to live! And what's even better is that God will give us the help we need to obey him.

Act It Out!

An Altar of Thanks

Materials
paper
pencils
chair or table (to be used as an altar)

Overview

Children draw pictures of what they are thankful for, and then lay it on the altar.

Preparation

Designate a table or chair to be Abraham's altar. For extra fun, have kids create an altar out of boxes.

Directions

1. Children write down or draw things on their paper that God has provided for them.
2. Children put their paper on the altar. They can share their answers with the class if they wish.
3. When the child comes up to the altar, they get to answer a **Talk about It!** question from page 41.

Conversation

After Abraham sacrificed the ram on the altar, he named the place The Lord Will Provide. Just as God provided the offering for Abraham's sacrifice, God provides for us. We need to thank God for his provision in our lives.

Play It!

Don't Make Me Laugh

Overview

A child must make the other children laugh. If someone laughs, they are out!

Directions

1. Children sit in a circle.
2. Select one child to be in the center. Their job is to make the other children laugh without touching them!
3. If a child laughs, they answer, or choose a volunteer to answer, a **Talk about It!** question from page 41. Then, they replace the person in the center.

Conversation

This was a fun, silly game, full of laughs. Who remembers what Isaac's name meant? Children respond. The name Isaac means he laughs. Sarah laughed at the idea of having a son when she was old, but God kept his promise.

Craft It!

Cotton Ball Rams

Materials

cardstock (1 per child)

markers

cotton balls (4–5 per child)

glue

Overview

Children make a ram with cotton balls.

Preparation

Print "God Provides" at the top of each paper.

Directions

1. In the center of the cardstock paper, children glue their cotton balls close together.
2. Children draw a ram's head, horns, and legs.

Conversation

Abraham was obedient to God, and God provided a ram for the sacrifice. Does God provide for us? Children respond. **Yes! We can thank God for all of the things he provides us with!**

Snack It!

Baby Cupcakes

Materials

mini cupcakes (1 per child)

Optional: birthday candles

Overview/Directions

Children eat cupcakes in celebration of baby Isaac's birth.

Conversation

We have birthday parties to celebrate our birthdays. At birthday parties, what do we have? Cake! Our snack today is cupcakes, which remind us of the celebration that went on when God's promise to Abraham and Sarah was fulfilled with the birth of Isaac!

Talk about It!

Basic Questions

1. How old was Abraham when Isaac was born? *100 years old.*
2. Who came to visit Abraham? *The Lord/Three visitors/angels.*
3. What did Sarah do when she heard she would have a son? *She laughed.*
4. Why did Sarah laugh at the news she would have a child? *Because she was so old.*
5. What did God ask Abraham to do with Isaac? *Sacrifice Isaac.*
6. What was Abraham's response to God's request?
   He willingly went to sacrifice Isaac.
7. When Isaac asked Abraham where the lamb for the offering was, what was Abraham's response? *That God would provide an offering.*
8. What stopped Abraham from hurting Isaac? *An angel.*
9. Was God pleased with Abraham's actions?
   Yes, because he was willing to sacrifice Isaac to obey God.
10. Did God provide the sacrifice? *Yes, a sheep was stuck in a bush nearby.*

Go Further

1. What were altars and sacrifices used for in Old Testament times? (See Hebrews 10:3.) *To remind the Israelites of their sins.*
2. What does it mean to FEAR the Lord?
3. Abraham placed his trust in the Lord, no matter what might have happened. Does anyone want to share a time when they trusted God like that?
4. What are some ways you can practice obedience to the Lord?

Wrap It Up!

God made a covenant with Abraham to make him into a great nation and to bless him with a son. God's promise was fulfilled with the birth of Isaac. Abraham was 100 years old (refer to the time line) when Isaac was born. Later, God tested Abraham, making sure that Abraham loved God above all. In his obedience to God, Abraham was willing to sacrifice his only son. No matter what, Abraham was willing to obey God. What a great example of obedience for us to follow!

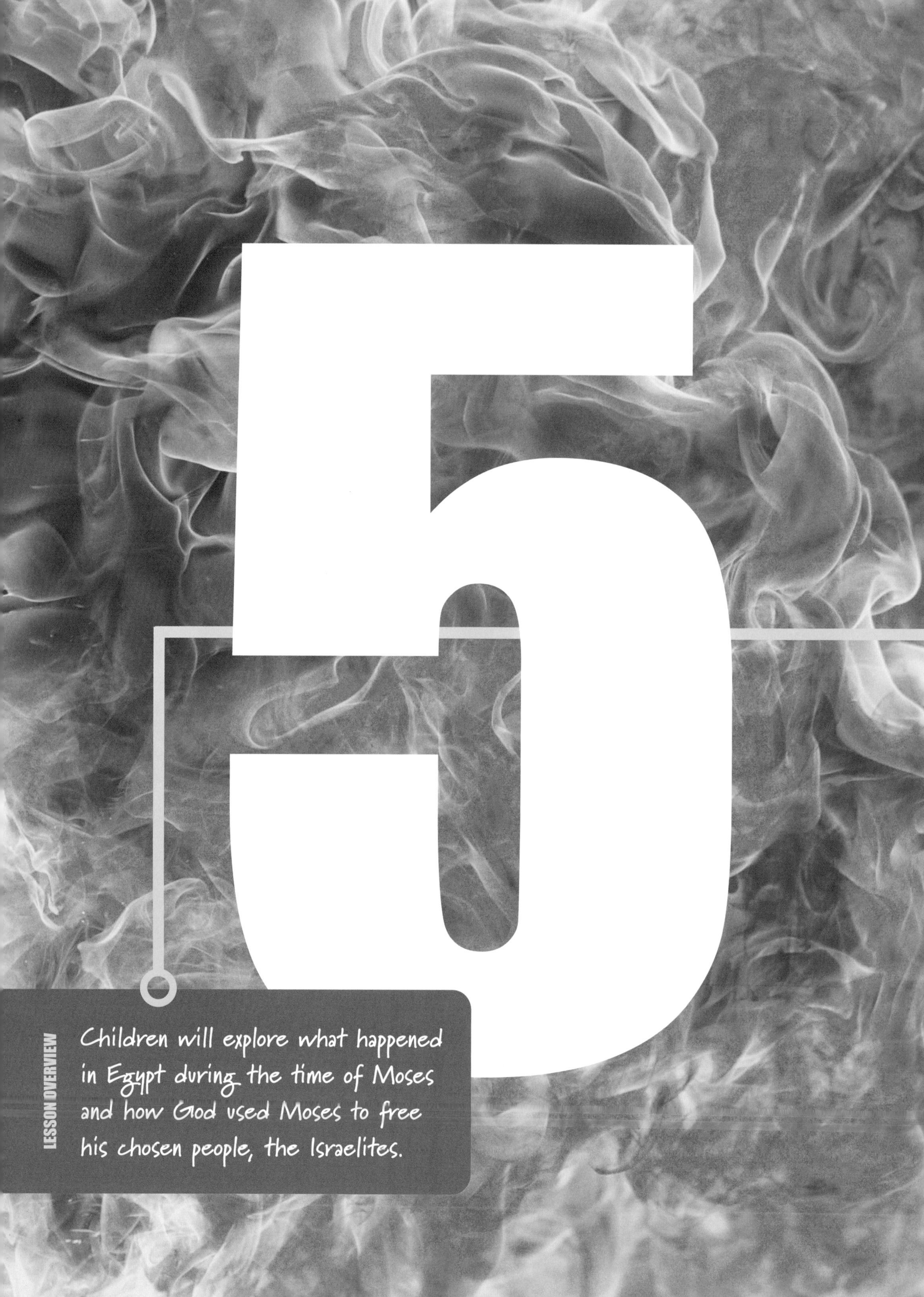
5
LESSON OVERVIEW
Children will explore what happened in Egypt during the time of Moses and how God used Moses to free his chosen people, the Israelites.

Moses

Exodus 1–5

Time Line

1500 B.C.

Key Events & People

God chooses Moses to free the Israelites enslaved in Egypt; Moses, Pharaoh

Memory Verse

This is my command—be strong and courageous! Do not be afraid or discouraged. For the LORD your God is with you wherever you go.

Joshua 1:9

Introduce It!

Time Line Materials needed. (See p. 4.)

#1

Begin the lesson in prayer. Thank God that he is always with us, wherever we go.

After many years, Abraham and Isaac passed away. Isaac's son, Jacob, lived in Canaan with his twelve sons. Place time line marker at 1900 B.C. Joseph was Jacob's favorite son, so he made him a beautiful coat. The other brothers were so jealous and angry that they sold Joseph into slavery in Egypt. Through hard work and God's grace, Joseph became governor of Egypt!

When a famine arrived, Joseph's brothers came to Egypt seeking food. Joseph forgave his brothers, and the whole family moved to Egypt. Place time line marker around 1876 B.C.

Joseph's family stayed in Egypt for a few hundred years. During that time, the Israelites grew and grew. Today, we are learning about an important Israelite named Moses.

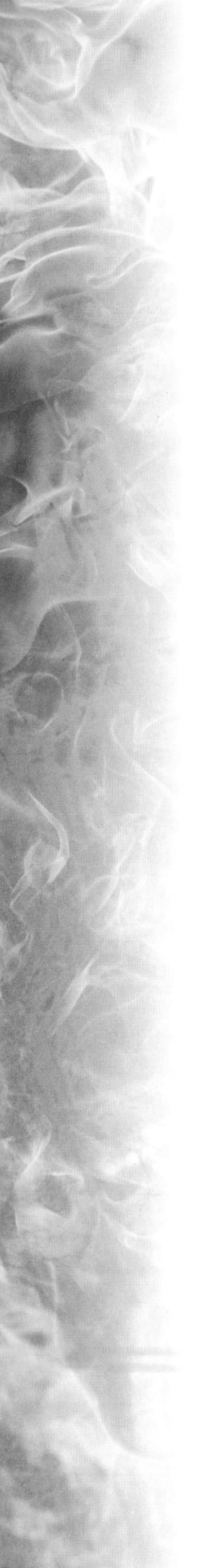

Tell It!

Choose a way to tell the story while reading the account from the Bible or telling it in your own words. Ideas for creative storytelling include acting it out, using props, or incorporating pictures.

Years Between Joseph and Moses

Moses was born at a dangerous time about 376 years after Joseph's family moved to Egypt. Place time line marker at 1500 B.C. Many pharaohs had ruled over Egypt since Joseph had been in power. They did not know about Joseph or how he had saved Egypt from famine (see Exodus 1:8). The new Pharaoh looked around and saw how many Israelites there were. He was worried that there would be more Israelites (God's people) than Egyptians (his people). So, he turned them into slaves. The Israelites were treated very harshly and forced to work.

Read Exodus 1:12–14.

Eventually, there were so many Israelites, Pharaoh ordered all of the Israelite baby boys to be thrown into the Nile River. God had not forgotten about his people, though. He had a plan for an Israelite to lead his people out of slavery.

A Baby in a Basket

One Israelite woman gave birth to a son, and she hid him from the Egyptian guards for three months. When she could not hide him anymore, she made a waterproof basket. She put the baby inside and hid him among the reeds. The mother told her daughter, Miriam, to watch the basket to see what would happen (see Exodus 2: 1–4).

Read Exodus 2:5–8.

The princess named the baby Moses. She paid Moses' mother to raise him until he was old enough to move to the palace.

Even though Pharaoh was having all of the Israelites' baby boys killed, God protected Moses. He had a plan for Moses to lead the Israelites out of Egypt.

Exodus 2:23 tells us that "the Israelites continued to groan under their burden of slavery. They cried out for help, and their cry rose up to God." Did God hear them? Children respond. Yes! God heard their cries, and their prayers, and he had a plan.

The Burning Bush

Perform the Won't Burn Up object lesson found on page 46.

WON'T BURN UP

Growing up, Moses knew he was an Israelite. One day, after he was a grown man, he witnessed an Egyptian slave master hurting one of his people. A flare of anger came over Moses. He killed the slave master and buried him the in sand. But Pharaoh discovered Moses's crime. He ordered Moses to be killed.

Moses ran for his life. He escaped to Midian and became a shepherd there. After a few years, he married a Midianite woman and had two sons. Moses spent his days watching the sheep, but one day, something strange happened in the wilderness.

Read Exodus 3:2–10.

God had heard the cries and the prayers of the Israelites. He wanted his people freed from Egypt, and he wanted Moses to lead them.

Pray It!

Dear God, thank you for always watching over me. Thank you for listening to my prayers. Even when I am scared, I know you are with me. In Jesus' name, amen.

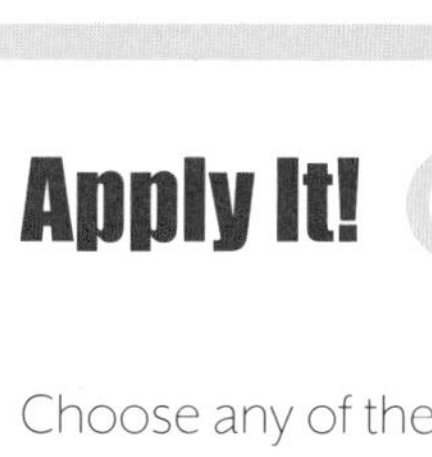

Apply It!

Choose any of these activities for your lesson. Use more than one if time allows. For any of these activities, discuss the **Talk about It!** questions on page 49 as time allows.

Show It!

Won't Burn Up

Materials

picture of a bush

shallow container (cooking pan, serving dish, storage container, etc.)

Isopropyl alcohol (91% rubbing alcohol)

water

salt

metal tongs

lighter

Overview

Light a solution-based paper on fire. Because of the solution, the paper will not burn.

Preparation

In shallow container, pour ½ cup Isopropyl alcohol, ½ cup of water, and ¼ teaspoon of salt. Do you think I can burn this picture of a bush without it burning up?

Directions

1. Soak the picture of a bush in the solution.
2. Pick it up with the tongs.
3. Light the paper on fire.
4. The alcohol will burn off the paper, but because of the water, the paper will not burn.

Conversation

Isn't that amazing? Imagine seeing a bush burning but not burning up. And that wasn't the most exciting part. God had a message for Moses. He told Moses that he had heard the cries of the Israelites. Moses was to go and tell Pharaoh to let God's people go!

Act It Out!

A Burning What?

Materials

burning bush prop; for example, a potted plant with red, orange, and yellow streamer "flames" tied on it.

Overview

Children act out reactions to the burning bush.

Directions

1. One at a time, children act out what their reactions would have been if they had seen God in a burning bush.
2. After all the children have a turn with their reactions, select a few children to act out Moses encountering God in the burning bush.

Optional

Use a burning bush prop for kids to react to. Or ask a volunteer to act like a burning bush and make burning noises.

Conversation

If we were to see a burning bush like Moses did, we might have some crazy reactions. The Bible tells us Moses saw the bush and then went to investigate. God called to Moses from the burning bush and told him about the job he had for him.

Play It!

Pyramid Stack

> **Materials**
> 20–50 disposable plastic cups per team

Overview

Children build pyramids out of cups.

Directions

1. Separate children into teams.
2. Demonstrate how to build a pyramid out of cups.
3. Teams race to create the best pyramid in the fastest time.
4. Team finishing first answers the **Talk about It!** questions on page 49 or recites the memory verse.
5. Repeat as time and interest allow.

Conversation

In this game, you were all racing to build cup pyramids. The Israelites were forced to build pyramids and work for the Egyptians, but it wasn't nearly as fun. Egypt wasn't a fun place for God's people to live in, but he had a plan to rescue them!

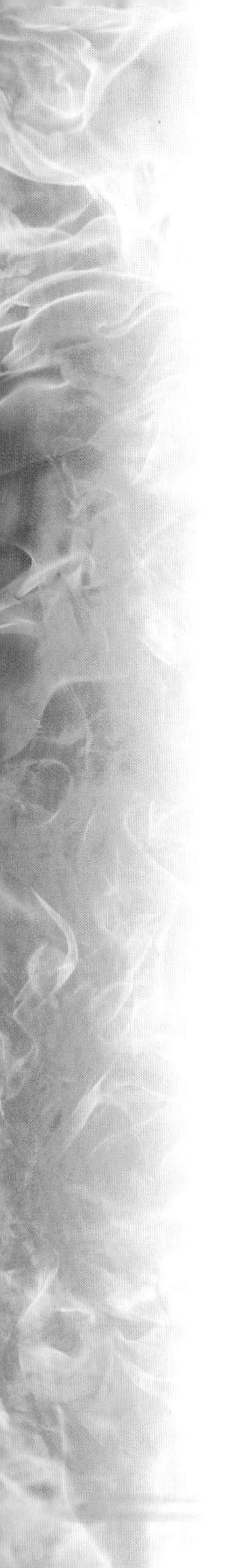

Craft It!

Prayer Bush

Materials

green paper cup (1 per child)

cardstock leaves (red, orange and yellow; 5–10 per child)

glue or glue sticks

markers

Overview

Children write prayers on paper leaves attached to a cup representing the burning bush.

Preparation

Cut out the leaves.

Conversation

What happened to Moses when he encountered the burning bush? Children respond. **He talked to God! For us, talking to God might not look like a burning bush. But when we pray, we are talking to God! God still talks to people today. To remind us of Moses talking to God and our talking to God today, you are going to create your own prayer bush.**

Directions

1. Hand out paper leaves to each child.
2. On each leaf, children write:
   - prayer requests
   - things they are thankful for
   - anything they would like to talk with God about
3. Help children glue the leaves onto their cups in a bush-like formation.

When all those red, and orange, and yellow prayer leaves are glued on, your prayer brush will remind you of Moses talking to God through the burning bush.

Snack It!

Basket Baby

Materials

fish-shaped crackers

pretzel sticks

paper cups

Overview

Children eat a snack that resembles the reeds and fish of the Nile River.

Directions

Children place fish-shaped crackers and pretzel sticks in a cup to enjoy as a snack.

Conversation

Does our snack remind you of anything we learned about in the story of Moses? Children respond. **The snack reminds us of when Moses was a baby. The pretzels look like the reeds that hid Moses's basket, and the goldfish remind us of the fish that swam underneath him.**

Talk about It!

Basic Questions

1. About how many years were there between Joseph and Moses? *About 400.*
2. How were the Israelites treated in Egypt?

   They were treated harshly because they were slaves.
3. Why did the Israelites become slaves?

   Pharaoh was scared of how many there were.
4. What rule did Pharaoh make so the Israelites could not take over?

   He had all Israelite baby boys killed.
5. How did Moses' mother keep him safe when he was a baby?

   She put him in a basket and hid him the in the reeds of the river.
6. Who found Moses in the basket? *Pharaoh's daughter.*
7. Moses was out tending his sheep and saw what crazy sight?

   A bush that did not burn up.
8. How did God speak to Moses? (See Exodus 3:1–10.) *Through a burning bush.*
9. What did God want Moses to do? *To tell Pharaoh to let God's people go.*
10. Did Moses want to go to Egypt and deliver his message? *No! He made excuses.*
11. What was Moses' response to the job God had for him? (See Exodus 3:11–12.)

    He asked why he was chosen to lead.
12. What was God's response to Moses' excuses?

    God told Moses to go, and that he would be with him.

Go Further

1. God spoke to Moses through a burning bush. How does God speak to people today?
2. Has God ever spoken to you? If so, were you willing to listen and obey? Do you think there is anything God could ask you to do that you do NOT want to do?

Wrap It Up!

Refer to the time line.

Wow, what an exciting time in Egypt and the Bible's history. In less than 400 years, the Israelites had moved to a new country (Egypt) and became oppressed slaves. They cried out to God for help. Since God is always in control, we saw that God had a plan. He saved Moses as a baby and used him to talk to Pharaoh.

6

LESSON OVERVIEW

God had a plan for Moses to free the Israelites from slavery in Egypt. Moses would lead the people to the Promised Land. At times, they struggled to trust God. Children see how God never abandons his people and how he took care of the Israelites.

Exodus 7—17; Numbers 20:6–12

Exodus & Wilderness Wanderings

Introduce It!

Time Line
1446–1406 B.C.

Key Events & People
The Exodus; Aaron, Moses, Pharaoh

Time Line Materials needed. (See p. 4.)

Begin the lesson in prayer. Thank God for always caring for us and for never abandoning us.

Moses has already been rescued as a baby in basket, fled to the desert, and encountered God in a burning bush. Though Moses wasn't sure he was the man for the job, he obeyed God. Now it's about 1446 B.C. (place time line marker at 1446 B.C.), and Moses is headed to Egypt with a message for Pharaoh.

Imagine if you were Pharaoh and in charge of a whole country. You have servants and slaves that do anything you tell them to do. If someone like Moses comes to you and demands you let your slaves go free, would you? What would your response be? Children respond.

God told Moses to tell Pharaoh to "let my people go!" (Exodus 9:1). Pharaoh had no plans of letting his slaves go. Scripture tells us that his heart was hardened. God, through Moses, gave Pharaoh ten chances to free his people.

Memory Verse

Be strong and courageous! Do not be afraid and do not panic before them. For the LORD your God will personally go ahead of you. He will neither fail you nor abandon you.

Deuteronomy 31:6

Play the Pharaoh Pharaoh activity found on page 55.

Tell It!

Choose a way to tell the story while reading the account from the Bible or telling it in your own words. Ideas for creative storytelling include acting it out, using props, or incorporating pictures.

Ten Plagues

When Pharaoh refused to let God's people go, a series of bad things happened each time:

- Blood—the Nile River turned to blood
- Frogs—thousands of frogs covered the land
- Gnats—everything was covered with gnats
- Flies—even more annoying
- Livestock—all the Egyptian farm animals died
- Boils—the Egyptian people were covered with painful sores
- Hail—people, animals, plants, and trees were damaged by an icy storm
- Locusts—plants were devoured by a swarm locusts.
- Darkness—a deep darkness fell on Egypt for three days
- Death of firstborn—the oldest son in every Egyptian home, both human and animal, died

Pharaoh refused to let God's people leave when each of the first nine terrible things happened. After the tenth and worst plague of death, Pharaoh finally said, "GO!"

A Path through the Red Sea

Moses led the Israelite people away from Egypt. They were finally free! But they didn't exactly know where they were going, and there was no such thing as a GPS! But God was with them.

Read Exodus 13:21.

God gave them the guidance they needed. By day, they walked, following a pillar of cloud! And at night, he provided them with a pillar of fire. This continued until one day when they realized they couldn't walk any farther. They had reached the Red Sea, which was too big to walk around or across. Even worse, Pharaoh had changed his mind and wanted the people to come back and be his slaves again! Pharaoh sent his army after God's people. They were stuck! The sea was in front of them, and Pharaoh's army was behind!

Read Exodus 14:15–28.

Manna and Quail

God performed amazing things in the presence of the Israelites. The ten plagues, the parting of the Red Sea, the pillars of cloud and fire, but the Israelites easily forgot that God was continually caring for them.

They had been wandering around in the desert on their way to the Promised Land, and they became hungry. They were so hungry that they wished they had died in Egypt!

How would you complain if you were hungry wandering around in the desert? Give me 10 seconds of your best hunger-complaints.

Read Exodus 16:3–5.

God made food fall from the sky—a food like bread! He promised that he would take care of the Israelites, and he answered their prayers. God knew that the people would get tired of bread, so he also sent quail for them to eat.

Read Exodus 16:13–15.

The Israelites had never seen food appear out of nowhere. They were so surprised. They called the bread *manna*, which means "what is this?" God gave the Israelites special instructions only to take enough for what they needed that day. They had to trust that he would provide for them.

Water from a Rock

God provided food for the Israelites, but as they traveled to the Promised Land through the desert, they began to complain and grumble again. They were thirsty!

Read Numbers 20:7–11.

Once again, God provided for the Israelites. But this time, Moses did not obey him. God said to speak to the rock, but instead Moses hit the rock. Because of his disobedience, Moses was not allowed to enter the Promised Land.

Pray It!

Dear God, help me to be strong and courageous. Remind me to pray when I feel scared. I know that you are always in control. In Jesus' name, amen.

Apply It!

Choose any of these activities for your lesson. Use more than one if time allows. For any of these activities, discuss the **Talk about It!** questions on page 59 as time allows.

Show It!

Feast of Tabernacles

Materials

tree branches (palm fronds, leafy branches, willow branches, etc.)

Overview

Children will hear a description of the Feast of Tabernacles, which is an annual celebration to remember how God cared for his people when they left Egypt.

The Bible tells us of many different kinds of feasts and holidays that people celebrated to remember important things that God did for them. One of these is the Feast of Shelters, also called the Feast of Tabernacles, or *Sukkot* (suh-KOHT) in Hebrew. Not only did God's people celebrate this feast in Bible times, but people celebrate it today!

Directions

1. Show tree branches. The Bible tells us God told his people to gather tree branches for a special celebration. Read Leviticus 23:39–43.
2. People gather to decorate small booths with tree branches and fruit. This reminds them of the tents the Israelites lived in while they were in the desert after leaving Egypt. The branches and fruit remind people of how God provided food and other care for his people. Traditionally, people live in the booths for the seven days of the celebration.
3. They also wave the branches in the air as a way to praise God as ruler over all the earth.

Conversation

We don't have to wait for a special celebration. We can praise God for his love and care every day! What is your favorite way to show God that you love him?

Act It Out!

Pharaoh, Pharaoh

Overview

Children act out the ten plagues.

Directions

1. Select a child to be Pharaoh and a child to be Moses. Everyone else is a Plague Player.
2. There are ten rounds to this game. Each round begins when Moses says, "Pharaoh, Pharaoh, let my people go," and Pharaoh says, "No."
3. Call out the corresponding plague for the Plague Players to act out. Children can make up their own actions or follow the suggestions below.
   - Round 1: Nile River turns to blood and all the fish die. Children pretend to take a drink, and then stick out their tongue.
   - Round 2: Frogs. Children hop or leap like frogs.
   - Round 3: Lice. Children scratch their heads.
   - Round 4: Flies. Children buzz around the room.
   - Round 5: All the animals die. Children make an animal sound, and then fall down dead.
   - Round 6: Sores and rashes break out the Egyptians' skin. Children make a disgusted face as they look at their arms and legs.
   - Round 7: Hail. Children cover their heads.
   - Round 8: Locusts eat all the crops. Children shove imaginary food in their mouths.
   - Round 9: Darkness. Children close their eyes and walk across the room.
   - Round 10: Death of first-born child. Children rock babies and pretend to cry.
4. Moses says, "Pharaoh, Pharaoh, let my people go," and Pharaoh says "Go!"

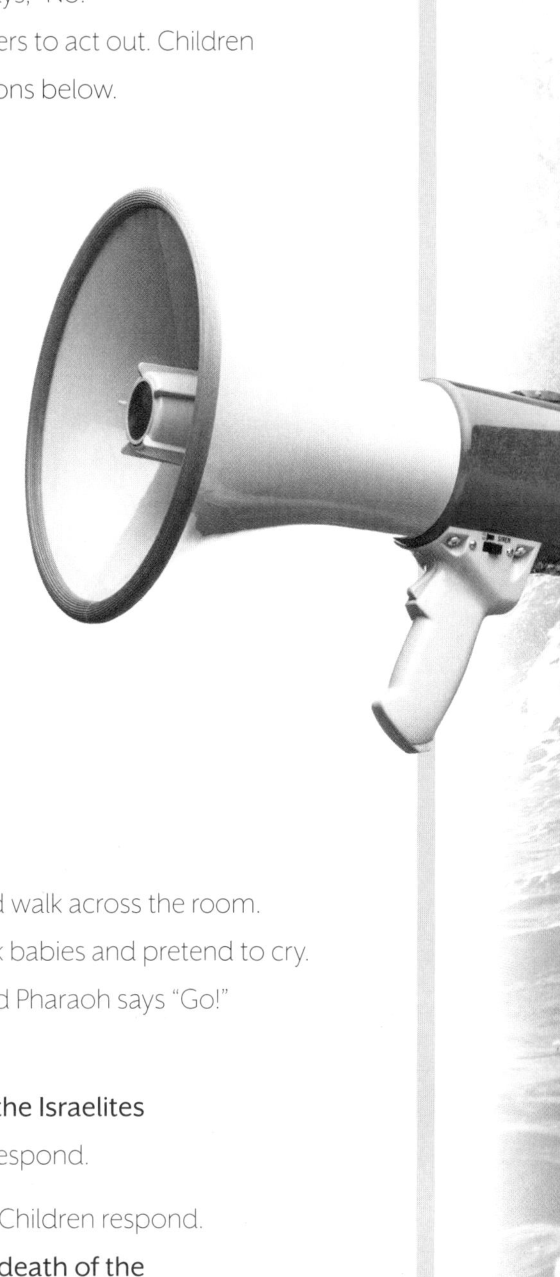

Conversation

God sent terrible plagues to convince Pharaoh to release the Israelites from slavery. Can you all name the ten plagues? Children respond.

Plague after plague, Pharaoh said NO until which plague? Children respond. **Pharaoh only let the Israelites go after the last plague, the death of the firstborn. The Israelites were finally free after 400 years of slavery.**

Play It!

Marshmallows from Heaven

Materials

miniature marshmallows

Overview

Children play a relay race to toss marshmallows into their partners' mouths.

Conversation

Every morning, the Israelites woke up to find bread from heaven! As much as they could eat. God provided for them. We aren't going to snack on manna from Heaven, but we are going to play a game called Marshmallows from Heaven. God provided food for his people, and we are going to provide a fun snack for our friends!

Preparation

Place two bowls of marshmallows on the other side of the room.

Directions

1. Divide children into teams.
2. Decide the first two players for each team. Assign one the role of thrower and one the role of catcher.
3. Say "Go," and two children from each team rush to their team's marshmallow bowl.
4. The thrower tosses a marshmallow into their catchers mouth.
    - If the catcher misses, try again until they do.
    - If the catcher catches it, the thrower runs back to the team and tags the new catcher. The old catcher becomes the new thrower and waits for the new catcher to arrive at the bowl.
5. Continue until everyone in the group has played.
6. Winners answer Talk About It questions from page 59.

Craft It!

Water from a Bottle

Overview

Children create a water bottle holder to remember how God provided water for the Israelites in the desert.

Preparation

Cut ribbon into 40-inch lengths, preparing one for each child.

Directions

1. Children cut adhesive-backed craft-foam sheets into rectangles to fit around their water bottles. Optional: Children decorate craft-foam rectangles with decorative materials.
2. Lay ribbon flat on table or floor. Stand water bottle in the center of the ribbon. Lift ends of ribbons and compare to make sure bottle is in the center. Adjust bottle placement as needed.
3. Lay ribbon back on table. Squeeze a line of craft glue along the ribbon where it will run up the sides of the bottle. (Be sure not to glue the entire ribbon!) Smooth ribbon up the sides of the bottle.
4. Tape each ribbon securely to the bottle until glue is dry.
5. Remove tape from bottle and the backing from the craft-foam shape you prepared and wrap it around the bottle. Press firmly in place.
6. Remove masking tape.
7. Tie ribbon ends into a knot to make a strap.

Materials

water bottles with straight sides (1 per child)

variety of adhesive-backed craft-foam sheets

scissors

pencils

craft glue

masking tape

variety of 1-inch ribbons

Optional: decorative materials (adhesive-backed craft-foam shapes, permanent markers, paint pens, etc.)

Conversation

I bet the Israelites worked up quite a thirst walking around in the desert. They didn't have a kitchen with running water or a store to grab a bottle of water from. During their journey, they even arrived at a place that had no water for them.

When we use our new water bottle holders and have our thirst quenched, we can remember how God met the needs of the Israelites when they were thirsty. Though they didn't have water bottles, God took care of them by providing water from a rock.

Snack It!

Manna Cookies

Overview

Eat vanilla wafer cookies to remember the manna God sent the Israelites.

Directions

Place a few vanilla wafers on a paper plate for each child to snack on.

Conversation

Is anyone hungry for a snack? The Israelites were hungry in the desert. When they got hungry, they started complaining. God provided for them, however. Every day, he sent manna down from Heaven to feed the Israelites. God was making sure their needs were met. He had not forgotten about his people.

Materials

vanilla wafer cookies or honey graham cookies

paper plates

Talk about It!

Basic Questions

1. Who did God send to tell Pharaoh to free the Israelites? *Moses and Aaron.*
2. Name the ten plagues. *Nile turns to blood, frogs, gnats, flies, death of livestock, boils, hail, locust, darkness, death of the firstborn.*
3. What did God provide for the hungry Israelites? *Manna and quail.*
4. What was the rule for keeping manna? *They could not keep any for the next day. It had to be eaten the day it was gathered.*
5. When the Israelites were thirsty, how did God provide for them? *Water came from a rock.*
6. How was Moses supposed to get water from the rock? *Speak to it.*
7. How did Moses disobey God while getting water from the rock? *He struck the rock with his staff instead of speaking to it.*
8. How long had the Israelites been slaves in Egypt? *About 400 years.*
9. How did the Israelites feel when wandering in the desert? What did they complain about? *Hungry, thirsty, annoyed. They kept complaining, saying they were better off in Egypt.*
10. Would Moses be allowed to enter the Promised Land? *No, he disobeyed God by striking the rock.*

Go Further

1. Moses disobeyed God by striking the rock instead of speaking to it. How was he punished? Does God punish sin?
2. What ways had God shown the Israelites he had not forgotten them?
3. How has God shown you he cares for you and won't forget you?

Wrap it Up!

For 400 years, God's people were slaves in Egypt. God had never forgotten his people. He sent Moses (refer to time line, 1446 B.C.) to free his people. Throughout their journey in the wilderness, God would show the people again and again that he did not and would not forget them. God is always in charge. He cares for his people, both Moses and the Israelites, and us today!

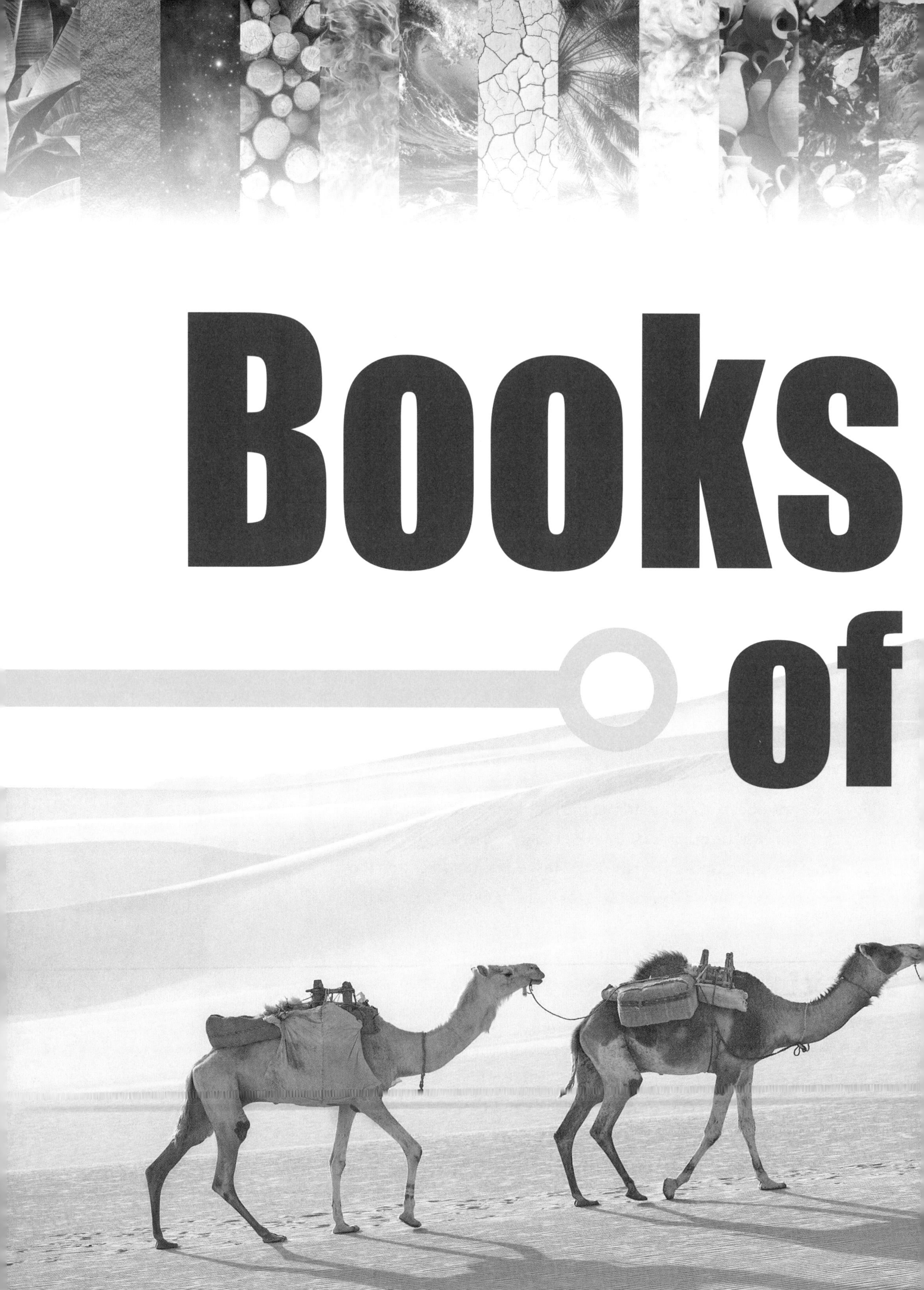
Books
of

HISTORY

7
LESSON OVERVIEW
Picking up right after the death of Moses, children will learn about Joshua, the new leader of the Israelites. God used Joshua to finally fulfill his promise to the Israelites and lead them into the Promised Land.

Numbers 13:27—14:35; Joshua 2–6

Joshua

Introduce It!

Time Line
1446–1406 B.C.

Key Events & People
Fall of Jericho; Joshua, Rahab

Memory Verse
Not a single one of all the good promises the LORD had given to the family of Israel was left unfulfilled; everything he had spoken came true.
Joshua 21:45

Time Line Materials needed. (See p. 4.)

Begin the lesson in prayer. Select volunteers to thank God for always being a promise keeper.

Make a list with the children, of promises that God has kept (both in the Bible and their lives).

After 400 years of being slaves in Egypt, Moses led the Israelites out of bondage. Refer to time line at 1446 B.C. **In just a short while, God has provided for the Israelites in some amazing ways: the plagues, the parting of the Red Sea, leading them by pillars of cloud and fire, sending manna from heaven, and creating water from a rock. God has promised his people that he would deliver them to a land that he had for them. A land flowing with milk and honey. The Israelites, it seemed, quickly forgot the promises God made to them, and about his constant care of them.**

Tell It!

Choose a way to tell the story while reading the account from the Bible or telling it in your own words. Ideas for creative storytelling include acting it out, using props, or incorporating pictures.

The Twelve Spies

Optional Materials

inflated purple balloons arranged on a pole like a bunch of grapes (so large you need two people to carry it)

If you moved to a new house, how would you choose which room is yours? Children respond. You'd explore the house to see all your options. The information you would discover would help you make the best decision.

When Moses and the Israelites neared the Promised Land of Canaan, they had to do some exploring, too. Moses sent out twelve scouts. When they returned, they had incredible news! Canaan was amazing. The fruit was huge! Two men had to tie a bunch of grapes to a giant stick and carry it between them. But there was a big problem, and the men were scared. Giants lived in Canaan, and there was a huge wall surrounding the city.

Ten of the twelve spies decided it was too risky to invade. These men, like most of the Israelites had quickly forgotten they had God on their side. But two spies, Caleb and Joshua, believed in God's power.

God was pleased with Caleb and Joshua, but he was angry with the rest of the Israelites. As punishment for their lack of faith, God did not let any of the Israelites of this generation enter the Promised Land, except for Caleb and Joshua. Because of their lack of trust, God sent the Israelites back to the desert to wander for forty years!

Rahab and the Spies

Move time line marker to 1406 B.C.

Fast forward to forty years later. God chose Joshua to lead the Israelites after Moses' death. Joshua sent two spies to check out the land of Jericho. The spies went into the city, but they had to hide for the night because the king of Jericho was looking for them. They met a woman

named Rahab, who agreed to help them hide in her house. Rahab hid the two spies on her roof. But why? Why would Rahab keep these two spies safe? They wanted to invade her homeland. Children respond.

Read Joshua 2:8–15.

Rahab saved the spies because she had heard the things God had done for his people. She believed in God. She helped the two spies escape from Jericho by helping them climb down the city wall using a red rope. The men promised Rahab that they would not harm her or her family when they invaded.

The Fall of Jericho

The land that God promised the Israelites was surrounded by a strong wall. But God did not leave the Israelites to figure out how to break the wall by themselves. He had a plan for the Israelites' victory. What was God's plan? Children respond.

Read Joshua 6:1–5.

What a crazy way to defeat a city's defenses! *"When the people heard the sound of the rams' horns, they shouted as loud as they could. Suddenly, the walls of Jericho collapsed, and the Israelites charged straight into the town and captured it. They completely destroyed everything in it with their swords"* (Joshua 6:20–21).

Though it was a little crazy, and not normally how you would bring down a wall, God's plan worked! The walls surrounding Jericho fell down! Joshua, through God's direction, led the Israelites into the land that had long been promised to them!

Pray It!

Dear God, thank you for always keeping your promises, even when things in life feel too big to handle. Help me to trust in your plan always. In Jesus' name, amen.

Apply It!

Choose any of these activities for your lesson. Use more than one if time allows. For any of these activities, discuss the **Talk about It!** questions on page 70 as time allows.

Show It!

Sounds of Breaking

Overview

Children imitate the sounds of things being broken while learning that God's promises can't be broken.

In today's Bible story, Joshua and the Israelite army made a mighty noise by playing trumpets and shouting. Then, God used his mighty power to break down the walls around Jericho. Those falling walls must have made an incredible racket!

Directions

1. One at a time, call on volunteers to think of a breakable object and then imitate the sound of the object breaking. The other children try to guess what the object was.
2. Next, call on volunteers to name things that cannot be broken.

Conversation

God had promised a special home for the Israelites—the Promised Land! He delivered the land to them when he broke down the walls of Jericho. Today's verse, Joshua 21:45 says, "Not a single one of all the good promises the LORD had given to the family of Israel was left unfulfilled; everything he had spoken came true." God always keeps his promises!

Act It Out!

The Walls Came Tumbling Down

Materials

party blowers (1 per child)

boxes stacked to resemble the wall

fake swords (optional)

Overview

As a group, the children will act out the different roles the Israelites had while marching around the walls of Jericho before the walls fell.

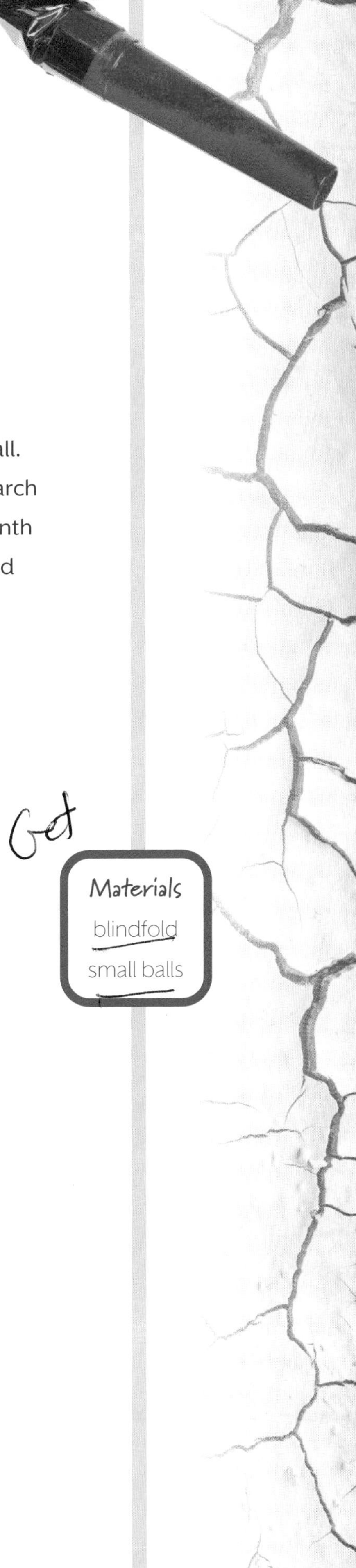

Directions

1. Stack boxes in the middle of an open area to symbolize a wall around Jericho.
2. Pass out party blowers and fake swords to the children.
3. Children march around the wall six times (one time per day), blowing their trumpets (party blowers).
4. On the seventh time, the children will run around the wall seven times while blowing their trumpets (party blowers). After they give a loud yell while knocking the boxes down.

Conversation

The city of Jericho seemed like a perfect place, one God had promised to the Israelites. One of the problems was that the city was surrounded by a strong wall. God had a plan for the Israelites to take over the city. He told the Israelites to march around the city once each day for six days, blowing their trumpets. On the seventh day of marching, they were to march around the city seven times and give a loud shout after the trumpet blast. After they did this, the walls of Jericho fell down.

We had to knock our box wall down. When the Israelites shouted after the seventh march on the seventh day, the walls came tumbling down. God fulfilled his promise to the Israelites to give them the Promised Land!

Play It!

Sneaky Spies

Materials
- blindfold
- small balls

Overview

Children try to sneak by a blindfolded giant and retrieve grapes (balls) to bring back to the start line.

Directions

1. Choose one child to be the giant. The giant will be blindfolded in the middle of the playing area, trying to tag any spies they can find.
2. The other children will sneak across the playing area, grab a grape (ball), and sneak back to the start line without being tagged by the giant.

Conversation

Joshua and the other eleven spies went into the land of Canaan to scout it out. They went to see how the land was and what it was like. Moses even wanted them to bring back some fruit from the land. Just like our game had a giant in it, the land of Canaan had real giants! There were great things about the land that God had promised them, but because of the giants and the strong walls, the people were afraid to take the land. They did not trust God to keep his promise.

Craft It!

Shout It Out Shofar

Materials

- shofar template
- construction paper or cardstock
- ruler
- scissors
- glue
- crayons or markers

Overview

Children decorate a shofar template with God's promises.

Preparation

Cut strips of construction paper or cardstock into 1x5 ½-inch strips.

Directions

1. Glue the shofar onto a piece of cardstock or construction paper.
2. With the pre-cut strips of paper, children write promises that God has made and kept.
3. Glue the promise strips on the paper like they are coming out of the shofar.

Alternate Idea

1. Children write promises that God made on a piece of paper.
2. Roll up the paper into a cone to resemble a shofar.
3. Children blow their new shofars.

Conversation

Trumpets, or shofars, can make a beautiful, but loud, noise! They can also be used to announce or introduce good news. We are using our shofars to shout out the promises that God has made and kept. He promised:

- A new land to the Israelites
- The strong walls of Jericho would fall down

What other promises did he make? Children respond. Great examples. We know that God kept his promises to the Israelites. And we know that he is still a promise keeper today!

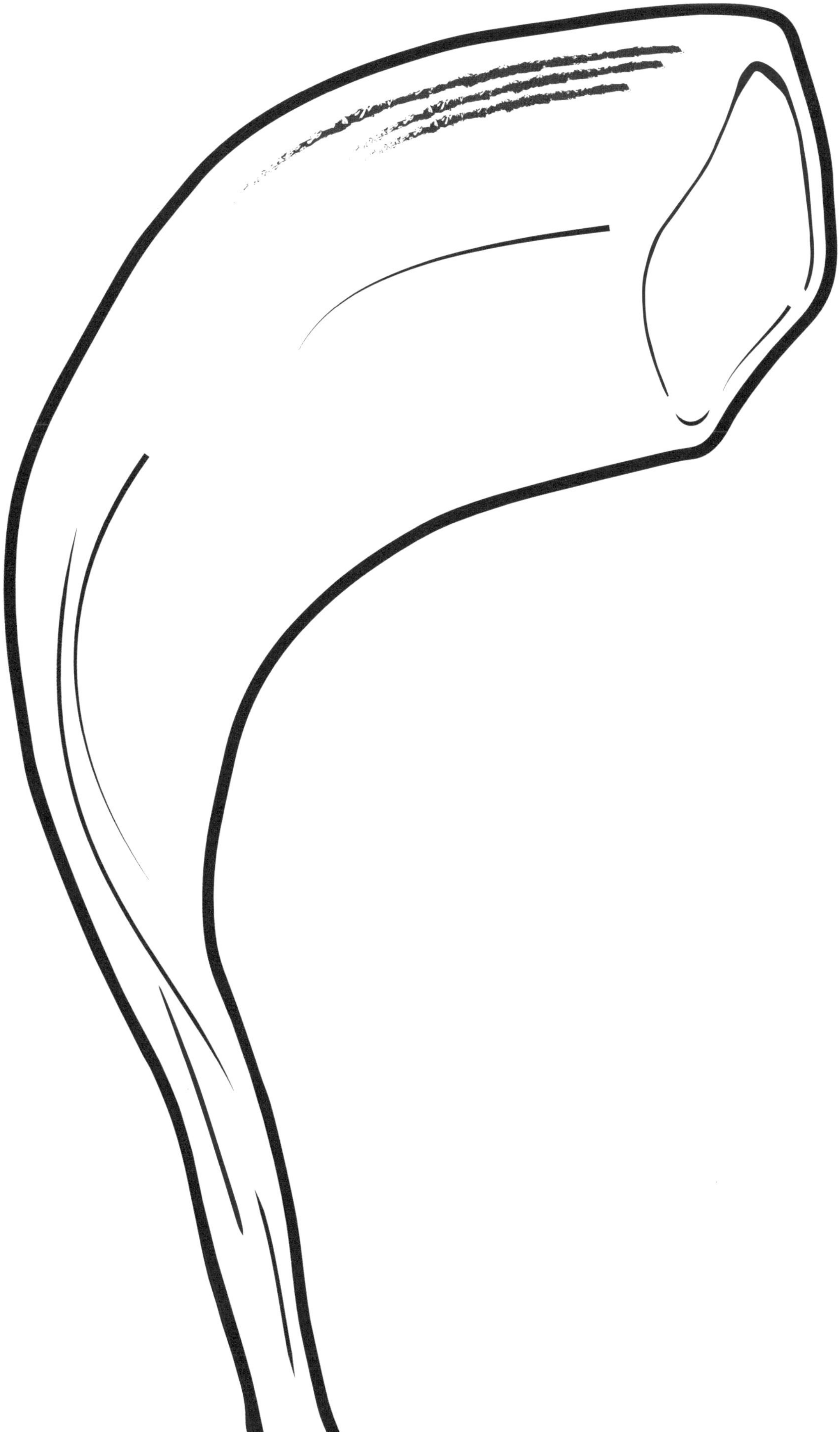

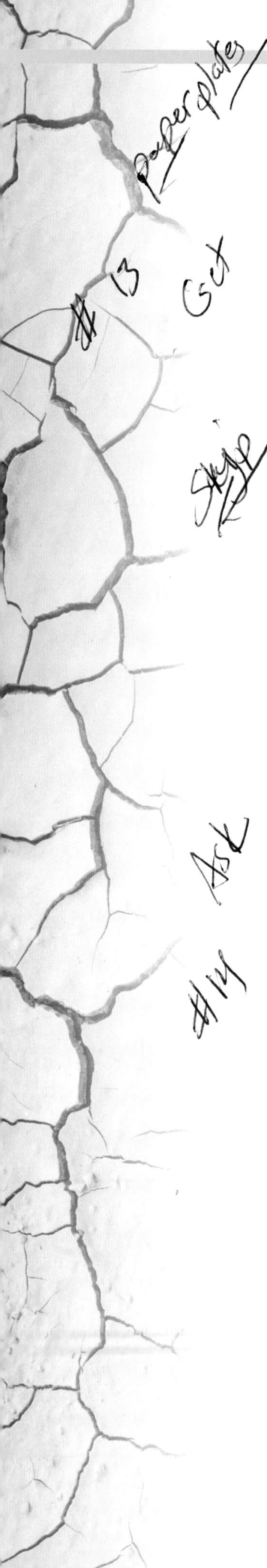

Snack It!

Gumdrop Walls

Overview

Children build a wall out of gumdrops and toothpicks as a reminder of Jericho. Then, they munch on Bugles corn snacks that represent the trumpets.

Materials

gumdrops

toothpicks

Bugles corn snacks

Conversation

The Israelites wandered in the desert for forty years. Under the leadership of Joshua, they finally arrived at the Promised Land, Canaan. The strong wall that protected the land was no match for God. God brought the walls of Jericho down and kept his promise to deliver them to the Promised Land!

Talk about It!

Basic Questions

1. When the twelve spies went to scout out the land of Canaan, what did they find? *A great land with lots of large fruit but also giants and a strong wall.*
2. When the Israelites first saw the Promised Land, did they want to attack? *No, they were scared.*
3. Which two spies were not scared but wanted to trust God instead? *Joshua and Caleb.*
4. What was the punishment for not trusting God and being afraid to enter the Promised Land? *They would wander for 40 years in the wilderness and not get to enter the land.*
5. How did Rahab keep the spies safe? *She hid them on her roof and helped them escape.*

6. Why did Rahab keep the spies safe? *She had heard about what God had done for the Israelites and she believed in God.*

7. What did the spies promise to Rahab in return for her helping them? *They promised to remember her and to keep Rahab and her family safe when they took over.*

8. What was God's plan for bringing down the wall around Jericho? *To march around the walls once per day for seven days and seven times on the seventh day. On the seventh time around, they would blow trumpets, shout, and the walls would fall down.*

9. What promise was fulfilled? *The Israelites conquered the Promised Land.*

Go Further

1. It took a long time for God's promise of a new land to actually happen. Does that mean God forgot about his promise? Why or why not?
2. If things are taking a long time in our lives, does that mean God has forgotten us? Why or why not?

Wrap It Up!

Refer to the time line.

The Israelites finally arrived in the land God promised them! Their forty-year punishment was over, and this new generation of Israelites was about to begin their lives in Canaan. God's promise was fulfilled! This promise started over 600 years before with Abraham. God promised Abraham that his descendants would be a mighty nation with a land of their own. God was talking about the Israelites. As Joshua led them into the Promised Land, we see the fulfillment of the promise that God made to Abraham.

8

LESSON OVERVIEW

Israel entered the Circle of Apostasy and the Era of the Judges. Sisera, the commander of an army with 900 iron chariots, attacked. Deborah became a judge of Israel and encouraged Barak to battle Sisera. After Sisera was defeated, Deborah ruled in peace for forty years.

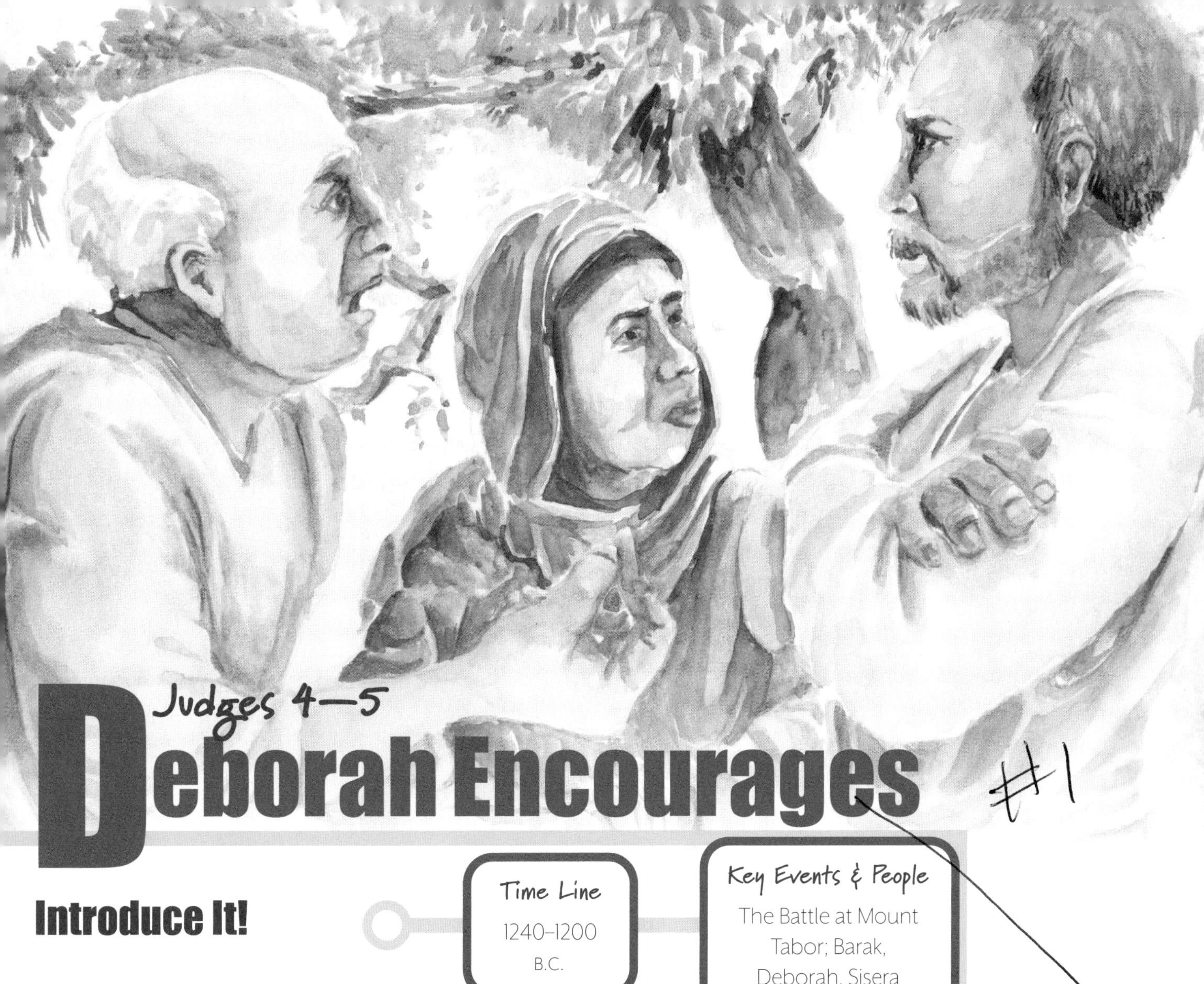

Judges 4—5

Deborah Encourages

Introduce It!

Time Line

1240–1200
B.C.

Key Events & People

The Battle at Mount Tabor; Barak, Deborah, Sisera

Time Line Materials needed. (See p. 4.)

Begin the lesson in prayer. Thank God for his continual forgiveness, like how he continually forgave Israel. Give the children a few moments to confess to God silently anything they need forgiveness for, reminding them that God always forgives our sins when we ask.

Memory Verse

Encourage those who are timid. Take tender care of those who are weak. Be patient with everyone.

1 Thessalonians 5:14

Just one generation after Joshua, the people did not know God or what God had done for their people. As punishment for no longer following God, the Israelites were handed over to their enemies. God no longer protected them from harm.

Then, out of the Israelites' distress, God raised up the judges. These judges were not like judges we see today. They were not like those on TV settling arguments and sending people to jail. These judges were the spiritual leaders for the people.

Read Judges 2:18–19.

The Israelites were stuck in the circle of apostasy for a few hundred years. *Apostasy* means that you abandon your faith. The Israelites' circle of apostasy went something like this:

1. The Israelites would stop following God and do evil in his sight.
2. God would punish them and let their enemies defeat them.
3. The people would repent and cry out for help.
4. Each time, God would raise up a judge to lead the people back to him.

> **Circle of Apostasy Sequencing**
>
> The Israelites REJECTED God. Make an X with your arms.
>
> The Israelites REPENTED. Spin around.
>
> God RESCUED the Israelites. Hold your hands in the air.
>
> The Israelites RETURNED to God. Jump backward.

Today we're going to discover the story of Deborah, the only female judge. Place time line marker at 1240 B.C. Deborah was judge over the Israelite people from about 1240 to 1200 B.C.

Tell It!

Choose a way to tell the story while reading the account from the Bible or telling it in your own words. Ideas for creative storytelling include acting it out, using props, or incorporating pictures.

Twenty Years of Trouble

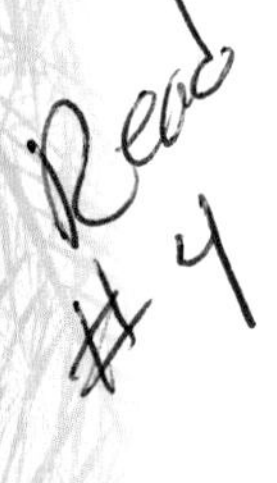

The Israelite people were in a time of terrible trouble. Once again, they had stopped following the one true God and begun worshiping idols, or false gods. And so for twenty years, they were under attack from a man named Sisera.

Read Judges 4:1–3.

Sisera's army had 900 iron chariots! The people were terrified! How could they possibly beat a man with 900 iron chariots? God heard the cries of his people. And he had a plan.

The Palm of Deborah

Deborah was Israel's judge. She would sit at a certain palm tree, listening to and settling the arguments people had with each other. Deborah trusted God and asked for his guidance to be a good judge. Deborah was also a prophet of God. A prophet is someone who God uses as a messenger. God had a message for Deborah to give his people about Sisera. What do you think God's message was? Children respond.

#5

A man named Barak (BEAR-uhk) was called to see Deborah. She said, "God has a job for you. You are to get 10,000 men to form an army and go to Mount Tabor. There, God will bring Sisera and his army. God will help you defeat Sisera!" How do you think Barak reacted to this plan? Children respond.

Barak was TERRIFIED! But he also wanted to obey God. He just needed some help from Deborah. Barak said, "Deborah, if you will go with me, I'll go. But if you don't go, I won't go either." Barak needed Deborah's encouragement to give him the courage for this important job. What do you think Deborah said? Children respond.

Barak may have been scared, but Deborah wasn't. "I will go with you," she said. So Barak sent messengers out to the Israelites, asking men to join his army, and Barak and Deborah headed to Mount Tabor.

The Battle at Mount Tabor

One day, Deborah told Barak that the time for the battle had come.

Read Judges 4:14. Rd #6

Barak was encouraged by Deborah's words and the knowledge that God would help him win the battle. So Barak and his 10,000 warriors came down the mountain. Closer and closer, they could see Sisera's chariots approaching across the dry and dusty valley. How do you think Barak and his men felt watching those chariots coming closer? Children respond. It must have been a terrifying sight! But they remembered Deborah's encouragement that God was with them.

Suddenly, there was a loud crash and lightning split the sky. It was a thunderstorm! Soon, water was everywhere. And the dry valley turned into mud—thick, sticky, gloopy mud. What do you think happened next? Children respond.

Sisera's chariots got stuck in the mud! When they saw Barak's army, they ran away! All Barak's army had to do was chase them far, far away. Soon, there was no one left to chase.

Deborah and Barak wrote a song about how God won this amazing battle. All the people sang praises and rejoiced that God had freed them from terror under Sisera. And they lived in peace and happiness for forty years. Deborah gave Barak the encouragement he'd needed to obey God and win the battle.

Pray It!

Do #7

Dear God, thank that you always send the encouragement we need to do your will. Thank you for always having good plans for us. We love you! In Jesus' name, amen.

Apply It!

Choose any of these activities for your lesson. Use more than one if time allows. For any of these activities, discuss the **Talk about It!** questions on page 81 as time allows.

Show It!

Paper Chains

Materials

toilet tissue or crepe-paper streamers

Overview

Children observe how something that is weak can be stronger when multiplied.

Our memory verse tells us that God wants us to encourage others, help the weak, and be patient with everyone. Watch to see something that's weak to begin with but becomes stronger with just a little help.

Directions

1. Choose a volunteer to hold their wrists together in front of them.
2. Wrap one strand of toilet paper around the volunteer's wrists. Challenge the volunteer to break free, which they will easily do.
3. Choose another volunteer, and this time, wrap the toilet paper around their wrists a few more times.
4. Continue for a few more rounds, each time adding more toilet paper, until it's very difficult or impossible for the volunteer to break free.

Conversation

One or two lengths of toilet paper can be pretty weak and easily broken. But the more toilet paper we add, the stronger it becomes. Sometimes, it can be easy to get discouraged when we're on our own. It can be hard to remember to trust God and accept his help. But when others join with us and encourage us, we become stronger! We can help others be stronger by encouraging them.

Act It Out!

Wheelbarrow Chariots

Materials
masking tape

Overview

Children act out the Bible story battle by pairing up to be a chariot and driver and then getting stuck in the mud.

Preparation

Mark the start line with masking tape. Make sure there is enough room behind the start line for all pairs of children. Ensure children have enough room to race in the playing area.

Directions

1. Children gather on one side of the playing area, form pairs, and get into wheelbarrow-race formation: One child stands in back and grasps the ankles of the other child who holds themselves up with their hands (in a push-up position).
2. On your signal, children then begin to race across the playing area.
3. When you say, "Thunder, lightning, and rain; oh my!" the children in front pretend to get stuck. Their partners then race back to the starting line. Once there, players recite the memory verse together.
4. Repeat, with children switching places.

Conversation

In our reenactment, it was funny when the chariots got stuck. But I'm sure Sisera and his men didn't think it was funny at all! God always has the most amazing ways of taking care of us.

But what if Barak hadn't been encouraged by Deborah to trust God? What if he just thought the job was too scary or too hard? Children respond. **God knows we need encouragement. That's why he gives us friends and family to be with us and help us be strong.**

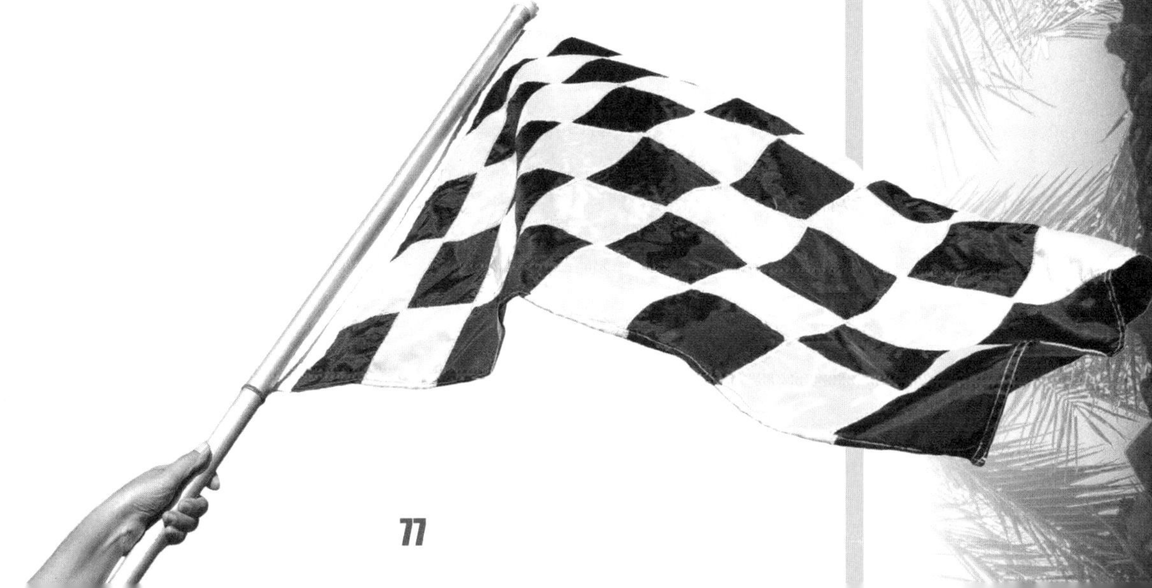

Play It!

Balloon Teamwork

> **Materials**
>
> balloons, one for every two children
>
> large plastic bag
>
> masking tape

Overview

Children work together in pairs to run a race carrying a balloon they can't hold with their hands.

Preparation

1. Inflate balloons and tie to secure. Place balloons in plastic bag.
2. Use masking tape to make a start line at one end of the playing area and a finish line at the other end.

Directions

1. Children form pairs and stand behind the start line. Give each pair a balloon.
2. Pairs take a few minutes to experiment with different ways to carry the balloon between them without using their hands. For example, pairs can carry the balloon between their heads, shoulders, elbows, hips, etc.
3. After pairs come up with their plan, they line up and race other pairs to the finish line. If you have enough pairs, you can put pairs in teams.
4. If a balloon is dropped, the pair must stop and position the balloon again. They can carry it the same way as before or try a new method for carrying the balloon.
5. The first pair or team to finish answers one of the **Talk about It!** questions on page 81.

Conversation

Could you have carried that balloon by yourself without using your hands? Maybe. It would have been even more difficult than it was with a friend. Friends can help us do difficult tasks by lending a hand . . . or a head, shoulder, elbow, or hip if hands aren't allowed. Raise your hand if your partner said anything to encourage you during the race. What were some of the encouraging things that were said? Children respond

Craft It!

Encouragement Bunting

Overview

Children decorate the room with a pennant banner that has encouraging words or phrases.

Materials

construction paper in a variety of colors

rulers

pencils

scissors

crayons or markers

decorative materials (glitter, stickers, craft-foam shapes, etc.)

crepe-paper streamer or yarn

transparent tape

Directions

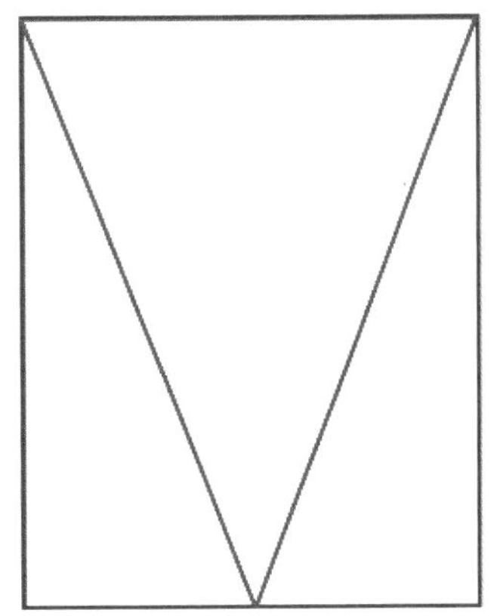

1. Children use rulers to draw pennant shapes on sheets of construction paper. Then they cut the shapes out.
2. On pennants, children write words, phrases, or sentences that can be encouraging to others: "Good job," "Thanks," "Keep it up," "You're good at that," "Please," etc.
3. Children use decorative materials and crayons or markers to decorate around the words, and then tape their pennant to a long length of crepe-paper streamer or yarn.
4. Children create as many pennants and banners as time allows.
5. Hang banners around the room as decoration that encourages.

Conversation

Whenever we read these encouraging words, not only will we feel encouraged, but they will be a reminder that we should encourage others.

Snack It!

Palm Tree Treats

Overview

Children make and then eat fruit laid out to look like a palm tree.

Materials

cutting knife (adult use only)
kiwis or green apples
bananas
oranges
paper or plastic plates

Directions

1. Slice bananas and kiwis or green apples and place in bowls. Peel and pull or cut oranges into sections. Place orange sections in bowls. Place bowls on tables where children will be working.
2. Make a sample snack for children to use as reference (see image).
3. Give each child a paper or plastic plate.
4. Children arrange fruit slices to make palm trees. When finished, children eat their palm tree snack.

Alternate Idea

Instead of bananas for the trunk of the palm trees, give each child a pretzel rod.

#12

Conversation

The Bible tells us that Deborah sat under a palm tree to listen to the problems the Israelites were having with each other. Our palm trees remind us that we can be like Deborah and encourage others.

Talk about It!

#13

Basic Questions

1. What was Deborah like? What are some words that describe her? *Judge. Prophet. Wise. Believer of God. Encourager to others.*
2. Why do you think Barak needed Deborah's help? *He was afraid. He didn't know if he could do what God wanted him to do.*
3. When God sent a storm, what happened? *Sisera's chariots all got stuck in the mud. Sisera's army ran away. The Israelites won the battle.*
4. When might it be hard for a kid to do what God wants? How could a friend help them to obey?
5. What something you know God wants you to do? *Be honest. Share with others. Stand up for others who need help.*
6. Who has helped you by encouraging you?
7. How could you encourage someone who has something difficult to do? *Pray for them. Say encouraging words to them. Lend a helping hand. Go with them.*

Go Further

Do as many as you can or they like.

#14

1. Deborah and Barak wrote a song to praise God for the amazing way he won the battle with Sisera. Singing this song was a great encouragement to all the people. Write a song about a way God has provided help and encouragement to you. Or write a song that could encourage someone going through a hard time.
2. Besides our memory verse, what are some other verses from the Bible about encouraging others? (See Romans 1:12, Romans 12:8, Ephesians 4:29, Hebrews 3:13, Hebrews 10:25, and 1 Thessalonians 5:11.)
3. Knowing how often God talks about encouraging others, how important do you think it is?

Wrap It Up!

#15

After the battle with Sisera, Deborah ruled as a judge over the people of Israel for another 40 peaceful years. However, the Israelites were not finished with the Cycle of Apostasy. Refer to the time line. Next time, we'll hear about one of the youngest judges, Gideon.

9
LESSON OVERVIEW
When God's people turn from him and fall into sin, the Midianites take over the land. They steal livestock and eat all the crops. God raises up Gideon, a lowly and insecure man, to defeat the Midianites in a way that shows God's power.

Judges 6—7

Gideon Trusts God

Introduce It!

Time Line

1137 B.C.

Key Events & People

Battle with the Midianites; Gideon

Memory Verse

Show me the right path, O LORD; point out the road for me to follow.

Psalm 25:4

Time Line Materials needed. (See p. 4.)

Begin the lesson in prayer. Thank God for the encouragement he gives us in his Word, the Bible, and for also giving us people who can encourage us.

The Israelites are still in the era of judges. After Deborah, the Israelites lost their faith again! Last time, we talked about the Circle of Apostasy. Let's do the motions we learned to review how the circle went around and around.

1. The Israelites REJECTED God. Make an X with your arms.
2. The Israelites REPENTED. Spin around.
3. God RESCUED the Israelites. Hold your hands in the air.
4. The Israelites RETURNED to God. Jump backward.

Place the time line marker at 1137 B.C.

We're now at 1137 B.C., about 213 years since the first four judges had been called by God. Today, we will learn about the fifth judge, Gideon.

Tell It!

Choose a way to tell the story while reading the account from the Bible or telling it in your own words. Ideas for creative storytelling include acting it out, using props, or incorporating pictures.

God Calls Gideon

Israel has been under the oppression of the Midianites for seven long years. It was so bad that the people started hiding out in caves and mountains. They cried out to God to save them, for him to raise up another judge. So God called Gideon.

Read Judges 6:14–16.

God had given Gideon a giant task. But he promised Gideon that he would be with him every step of the way! Still, Gideon was scared. He wanted to double and triple check that God really was going to be with him during this big job.

Gideon asked for a sign—something only God could do. He put a dry piece of wool outside. He asked God to make it wet with dew in the morning, but to keep the ground around it dry. Sure enough, the next morning the fleece was wet and the ground dry. Not only was the fleece wet, but it was so wet that Gideon was able to squeeze a whole bowl full of water from it!

God gave Gideon the sign that he asked for, but Gideon was still unsure that God would be with him. He asked for another sign.

Perform the Dry Fleece object lesson on page 86.

DRY FLEECE

Read Judges 6:39–40.

God showed Gideon yet again that he would be with him to defeat the Midianites.

Gideon Defeats the Midianites

Now that Gideon was absolutely positive that God had spoken to him, he assembled his army. Gideon had an army of 32,000 men. God told him that was too many men. Why do you think God said that? Why is it a bad thing to have too many soldiers? Children respond. God did not want the Israelites to brag, thinking that they defeated the Midianites. The glory was God's, so he started sending men away. How do you think God decided who should go? Children respond.

First, God told Gideon to send away any man that trembled with fear. Twenty-two thousand men went home. Gideon only had 10,000 left, but God said that was STILL too many. This time Gideon took the men down to the water to drink. Can you all show me how you'd drink water from a river? Children act it out. God said if the men lapped the water up like a dog, they went home. If they scooped up the water with their hands, they stayed. Three hundred men stayed.

Read Judges 7:16–21.

From an army of 32,000, God chose just 300 men armed with trumpets and jars to defeat their powerful enemy. Without God, there was no way Gideon and his men could have won. God was with them, and just as he promised, the Midianites were defeated!

Pray It!

Dear God, when things in life are going well, it's easy to forget to pray. Help me to remember to thank you every day for the things you have blessed me with. In Jesus' name, amen.

Apply It!

Choose any of these activities for your lesson. Use more than one if time allows. For any of these activities, discuss the **Talk about It!** questions on page 90 as time allows.

Show It!

Dry Fleece

Materials

small glass jar/cup

washcloth

container of water

Note: the water level in the container needs to reach over the glass.

Overview

A simple science experiment using a piece of cloth reminds children of Gideon's fleece.

Directions

1. I am going to place this cloth into the water without it getting wet. Do you think I can do it? Children respond.
2. Place the cloth at the bottom of the empty jar.
3. Tip the jar upside down. Make sure the cloth stays in the bottom of the jar.
4. Without tilting the glass, lower the upside-down glass (with cloth in the bottom) into the container of water.
5. Lift the glass out of the water the same way without moving it side to side. Due to the air pocket it creates, the cloth will come out dry.

Conversation

The cloth went into the water but did not get wet. Pretty cool! This was just a science trick, though. I did not need any special powers to make it happen, just simple science.

Act It Out!

'Round and 'Round They Go

Materials

4 sheets of paper

pen

tape

Overview

Children play a game like Four Corners to learn the Circle of Apostasy.

Preparation

1. Write the following words on three separate sheets of paper: REJECTED, REPENTED, RESCUED, RETURNED.
2. Tape each piece of paper to one corner in the room.

Directions

1. Children move to each corner as the trigger word is read in the following story.
2. When children get to the corner, they do one of the following motions:

- REJECTED: Make an X with your arms.
- REPENTED: Spin around.
- RESCUED: Hold your fists in the air.
- RETURNED: Jump backward.

God sent many judges to help the Israelites turn back to him. The Israelites did evil and REJECTED the Lord. After eight years of slavery, they REPENTED and cried out to God. God sent Othniel as judge. Othniel RESCUED the Israelites. They RETURNED to God and enjoyed 40 years of peace.

Then the Israelites did evil things again and REJECTED God. They were oppressed by the King of Moab for 18 years before they REPENTED. God called up Ehud, who RESCUED the people. The Israelites RETURNED to God for 80 years of peace.

The Israelites once again REJECTED God. He called up Shamgar when they REPENTED. The Bible doesn't say much about him, but he helped RESCUE the Israelites. Then they RETURNED to God.

Again, the Israelites did evil and REJECTED God. God called up the only female judge. Do you remember her name from our last lesson? Children respond. Deborah! The Israelites REPENTED and Deborah RESCUED the people. They RETURNED to God for 40 years of peace.

The next judge is Gideon, let's see if you can say and do the Circle of Apostasy on your own now.

3. Children respond and complete the circle by going around the room.

Conversation

Great job, everyone! The Israelites continued to reject God, and he continued to send them judges. While the judges were alive and leading Israel, the people followed God. The very last judge was Samuel, who we will learn about in our next lesson.

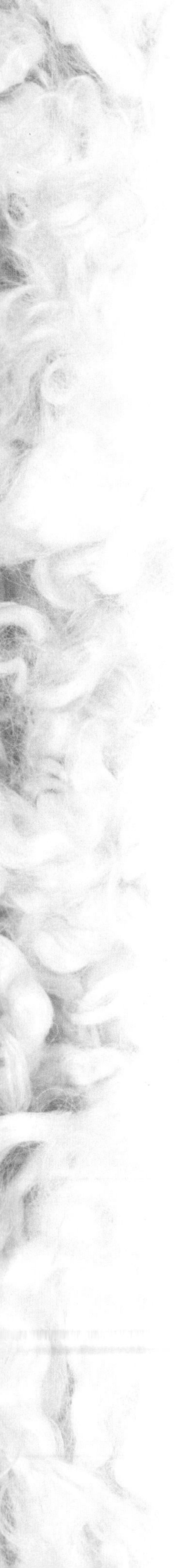

Play It!

Blind Man's Bluff

Materials
blindfold

Overview

A blindfolded child wanders around the room trying to tag other players who are frozen in place. Emphasizes that we can't see God, but we know he is always present.

Directions

1. Blindfold the designated "It" player.
2. Spin "It" around in the center of the room while other children walk around the room.
3. Stop spinning "It."
4. Other children continue to walk around the room until "It" says "FREEZE!"
5. "It" wanders around the room trying to tag the other children. The other children may bend or lean out of the way, but they cannot move their feet. If they move their feet, they are out.
6. Game continues until all players are tagged.

Tips

- Every time someone is tagged by "It," let "It" know how many players are left.
- If "It" gets really stumped, announce that the children still playing must move around for five seconds. "It" cannot move during that time but should be listening for where the other children are. After five seconds, everyone freezes in a new position. "It" resumes wandering.

Conversation

Ask the blindfolded child: **While you were playing the game, did it ever feel like someone was standing beside you, but when you reached out, there was no one there?** Child responds. **It's frustrating, right?**

Imagine that you have to do something big. Let's say you have to speak in front of the whole church. You would feel better if someone was there with you, right? Children respond. **God is always with us, even when we can't feel him near. Gideon was very nervous to fight the Midianites. Twice, he asked God to prove that he was with him. That's how scared he was. But God was with him the whole time.**

Craft It!

Flames of Victory

Overview

Children make a tissue-paper torch and write the memory verse along the handle.

Materials

red, orange, and yellow tissue-paper

scissors

ruler

markers

craft glue

paper-towel tube (1 per child)

Preparation

- Cut yellow tissue paper into approximately 1-foot by 1-foot squares, making one for each child.
- Cut orange tissue paper into approximately 10-inch by 10-inch squares, making one for each child.
- Cut red tissue paper into approximately 9-inch by 9-inch squares, making one for each child.

Directions

1. Write the memory verse on the paper-towel tube.
2. Layer the tissue paper on top of each other with the yellow at the bottom, the orange in the middle, and the red on top.
3. Pinch the center of the tissue paper and pull up.
4. Continue to pinch and twist the end of the tissue-paper until you have a little handle. This is your flame.
5. Apply glue to the top of the paper-towel tube.
6. Push the tissue-paper handle inside the tube. Hold for a minute until glue dries.

Conversation

Gideon was worried about fighting the Midianites. Their armies were so huge that they were eating up all the food and resources in Israel. But God had a plan. He wanted his people to remember his power. So he picked only 300 soldiers to surround the enemy camp. Then they held up their torches and they blew their trumpets. The Midianites were so scared! God's people won the battle. Let's be like Gideon. Hold up your torches and make a trumpet sound with your mouth. Children follow along. **God always has a plan, and he always saves his people.**

Snack It!

Kid Kabobs

Overview

Children skewer snacks in a repeating pattern to remember the circle of apostasy.

Preparation

Place bite-sized snack foods in bowls and place where children can reach them.

Materials

bowls

bite-sized snack food (grapes, berries, cheese squares, ham chunks, olives, tomatoes apples, marshmallows, etc.)

wooden skewers or lollipop sticks

Directions

Children place bite-sized snacks on their skewers in a repeating pattern. And then eat their snacks.

Conversation

Who thinks they have the best pattern of snacks on their skewers? Children respond. **We placed food on our skewers in a repeating pattern to remind us of the era of judges and the bad pattern the Israelites were in. The Israelites kept going through the pattern, the circle of apostasy.**

Talk about It!

Basic Questions

1. **When the Israelites did evil in the eyes of the Lord, what happened?** *God stopped protecting them from their enemies.*
2. **What was the role of the judges?** *To lead the people spiritually.*
3. **What are the four parts to the circle of apostasy?** *The Israelites REJECTED God. The Israelites REPENTED. God RESCUED the Israelites. The Israelites RETURNED to God.*

4. What kind of test did Gideon ask God to perform to prove that he wanted Gideon fight the Midianites? *To have wet fleece and dry ground, and then dry fleece and wet ground.*
5. How many men did Gideon start with in his army? *32,000 men.*
6. Why were 32,000 men too many? *God wanted the glory, not Israel.*
7. How many men left because of fear? *22,000.*
8. What was the second test to lower the number of soldiers? *If they lapped the water like a dog, they were sent home. If they cupped their hands to drink, they stayed.*
9. How many men did God leave Gideon with to fight? *300 men.*
10. What three things were the men armed with? *Trumpets, torches, and jars.*

Go Further

1. After all of the amazing things God had done and continued to do for the Israelites, why do you think they had such a hard time following him?
2. God sent the judges to help Israel follow him. What do we have that can help us follow him? *The Bible, the Holy Spirit.*
3. After we sin, can our sins be forgiven? How? (See 1 John 1:9, John 3:16.)

Wrap It Up!

Refer to the time line.

Gideon was unsure of himself when God called him to be a judge, but God promised that he would be right beside him. Through God, Gideon defeated the Midianites with a small army using trumpets and jars. For forty years, the Israelites enjoyed peace under Gideon's guidance. Unfortunately, the peace did not last. The Israelites had not learned their lesson, and after Gideon's death, the Israelites stopped following God once again. The circle began all over again, until God called the next judge to lead the people.

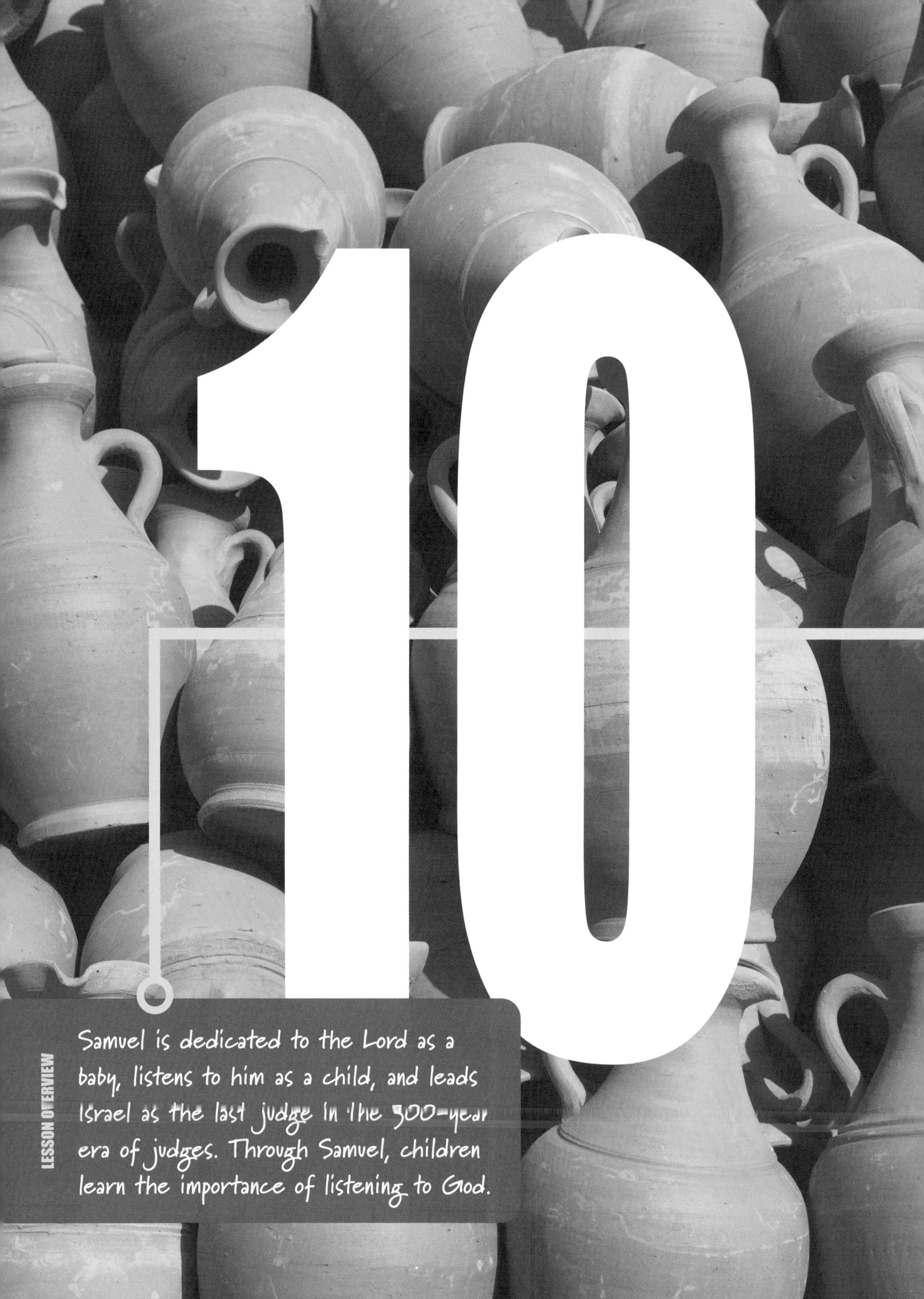

10

LESSON OVERVIEW

Samuel is dedicated to the Lord as a baby, listens to him as a child, and leads Israel as the last judge in the 300-year era of judges. Through Samuel, children learn the importance of listening to God.

1 Samuel 1,3,8—10

Samuel Listens

Introduce It!

Time Line

1060–1020 B.C.

Key Events & People

Samuel's birth,
Saul's anointing;
Eli, Samuel, Saul

Time Line Materials needed. (See p. 4.)

Begin the lesson in prayer. Thank God for the encouragement he gives us in his Word, the Bible, and for also giving us people who can encourage us.

Memory Verse

Serve only the LORD your God and fear him alone. Obey his commands, listen to his voice, and cling to him.

Deuteronomy 13:4

Last time, we talked about Gideon, one of the judges over the Israelites. All through the era of the judges, God's people were stuck in what we refer to as the Circle of Apostasy. Let's do our motions to remind us how the circle goes.

1. The Israelites REJECTED God. Make an X with your arms.
2. The Israelites REPENTED. Spin around.
3. God RESCUED the Israelites. Hold your hands in the air.
4. The Israelites RETURNED to God. Jump backward.

Unfortunately, the people STILL kept disobeying—rejecting, repenting, getting rescued, and returning to God. Today we are at the end of the era of the judges, at around 1060 B.C. (place time line marker at 1060 B.C.), when the very last of Israel's judges was about to be born.

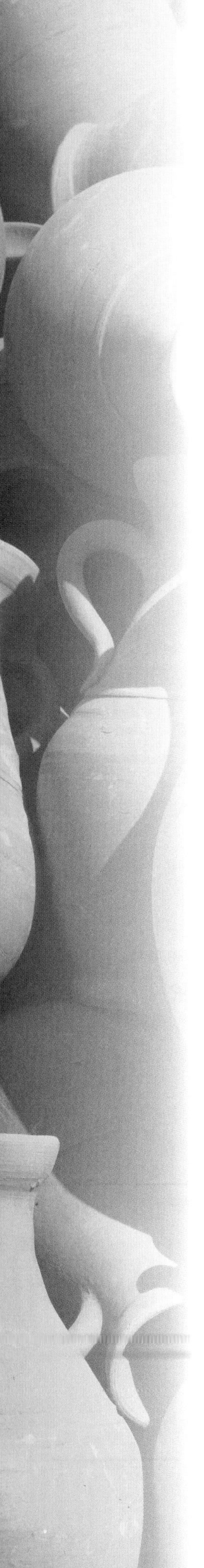

Tell It!

Choose a way to tell the story while reading the account from the Bible or telling it in your own words. Ideas for creative storytelling include acting it out, using props, or incorporating pictures.

Hannah Prays for a Baby

Have you ever really, really, really wanted something? Children respond. **Once there was a woman named Hannah, and she really wanted a baby. She was so upset that she wouldn't eat. She went to the Tabernacle (the place of worship) and cried loudly. She was so desperate for a baby that she made a strange promise to God.**

Read 1 Samuel 1:11.

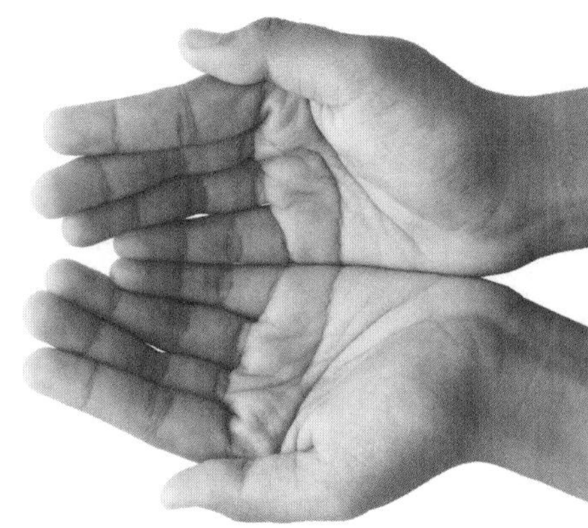

Hannah promised that if God would bless her with a child, she would dedicate her child to God. The child would serve God for their whole life. God heard Hannah's prayer. Soon, she became pregnant and gave birth to a son. She was so happy! She named her son Samuel, which means "God heard."

When he was old enough, Hannah took Samuel to the house of the Lord, just as she had promised. Samuel began training under Eli, the priest.

God Calls Samuel

Samuel was asleep in the house of the Lord. Suddenly, he heard someone call his name. He thought it was Eli. Maybe Eli needed something. Samuel got up and went to Eli's room.

"What do you need?" Samuel asked.

"I didn't call you; go back to bed," said Eli. Samuel obeyed and went back to bed. Again, Samuel heard his name called. He jumped out of bed and ran to Eli. Again, Eli told him to go back to bed. It happened a third time, and finally Eli realized what was going on.

Read 1 Samuel 3: 8–9.

God was calling Samuel!The fourth time God called, Samuel answered. God told Samuel that Israel was going to be punished because Eli's sons had disobeyed God. God had warned Eli about this, but he did not do anything about it. When Eli heard the news, he said, "Let [God] do what he thinks is best" (1 Samuel 3:18).

Samuel Anoints Israel's King

When Samuel grew up, he became a judge over Israel. He also appointed his sons to be judges over Israel, but unlike Samuel, they were harsh and greedy. The era of judges had lasted for almost 300 years, and the Israelites decided they wanted a king instead of a judge. All the nations around them were led by kings, and they wanted one, too.

At first Samuel was upset. He felt the people were rejecting him as a leader. God told Samuel he wasn't the one being rejected. Instead, the people were rejecting God. He told Samuel that he had picked a king for Israel.

Read 1 Samuel 9:15–21.

God had picked Saul to be the new king, even though he was from the smallest tribe of Israel.

Read 1 Samuel 10:1.

Even though God wanted to remain king over Israel, he heard the Israelites' cry. Samuel listened to God's words and obeyed him. He appointed Saul as king over all of Israel. All the people cheered "Long live the king!"

Pray It!

Dear Lord, sometimes it is difficult for me to hear your voice. I have so much going on in my head, and it's hard to focus. Please help me to be still. Teach me how to be a good listener. In Jesus' name, amen.

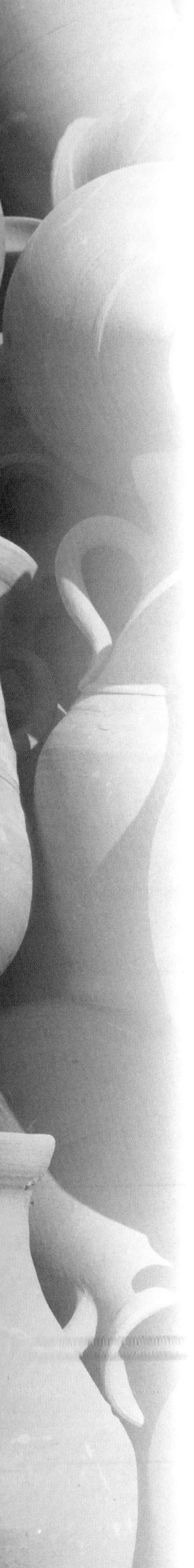

Apply It!

Choose any of these activities for your lesson. Use more than one if time allows. For any of these activities, discuss the **Talk about It!** questions on page 99 as time allows.

Show It!

Materials

several objects that make identifiable sounds (stapler, bell, squeaky toy, noise-maker novelties, kids' meal toys with sound effects, tambourine, maracas, etc.)

big, deep box

What Do You Hear?

Overview

Children listen to sounds and try to guess what they are.

Preparation

Place items in box.

Directions

1. Place big box of items on a table in front of you. Ensure that the children cannot see inside the box.
2. In the mystery box, keep your hands hidden from children and use item to make the sounds one at a time. For each one, children guess what the sound is.

Alternate Idea

Play sound effects on your phone.

Conversation

You had to listen carefully, right? Do we ever need to listen to God? Children respond. **Yes! God talks to us, and we need to be ready to listen to and follow what he says!**

Act It Out!

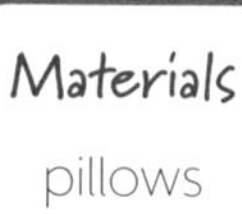

Materials

pillows

blankets

The Calling of Samuel

Overview

Children re-enact God calling Samuel.

Directions

1. Select a child to play Samuel and one to play Eli. These children will need to learn a line. Samuel will say, "Here I am," and Eli will say, "I did not call you; go back to bed." A leader will read the voice of God.
2. The children playing Eli and Samuel should lie down and pretend to sleep.

3. Follow this simple script to act out the Biblical account.

God: Samuel!

Samuel: Here I am. Did you call me?

Eli: I did not call you. Go back to bed.

God: Samuel!

Samuel: Here I am. Did you call me?

Eli: I did not call you. Go back to bed.

God: Samuel!

Samuel: Here I am. Did you call me?

Conversation

Until that special night, Samuel had never heard God speak. He didn't recognize God's voice. God had to call him four times before he finally said "Speak, your servant is listening." God had a special message for Samuel to hear and a job for Samuel to do.

Play It!

Listen Up

Overview

Children listen to instructions for teaming up with a partner.

Directions

1. Instruct the kids to walk around the playing area.
2. A leader will call out two body parts. The goal is to find a partner and match what is called, (i.e. back to back, thumb to thumb, etc.)
3. The last pair to match up is out.

Conversation

How did you know what you were matching up in the game?

Children respond. You had to listen to my voice!

Samuel listened to God's voice when he called him, and Samuel continued to follow God as he grew. The same is true with us. We know what to do in life by listening to God's voice and following what he says.

Craft It!

Color Instructions

Overview

Children listen to instructions as they color a picture.

In today's Bible story, Samuel thought Eli was calling him in the middle of the night. But it wasn't Eli! Eli told Samuel it must be the Lord who was calling him. When God called Samuel again, Samuel replied, "Speak, your servant is listening" (1 Samuel 1:10). Let's practice listening as we color a picture.

> **Materials**
>
> coloring page (1 per child)
>
> crayons or markers
>
> **Note:** Though you can use any coloring page, we suggest the coloring page for this story at the back of the book.

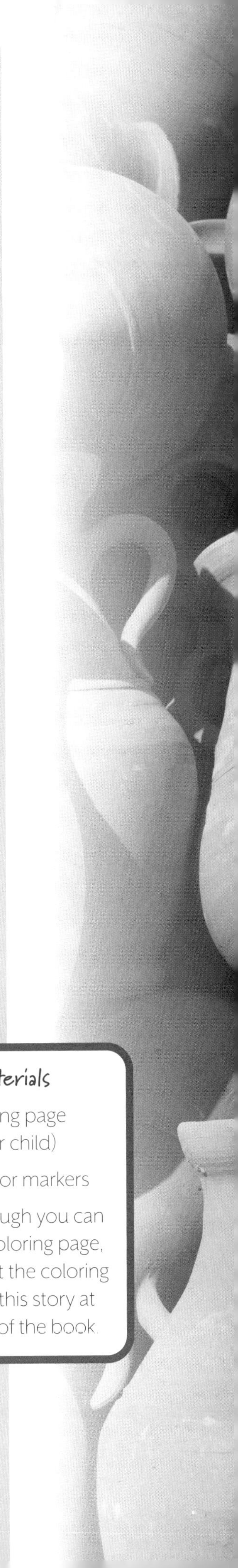

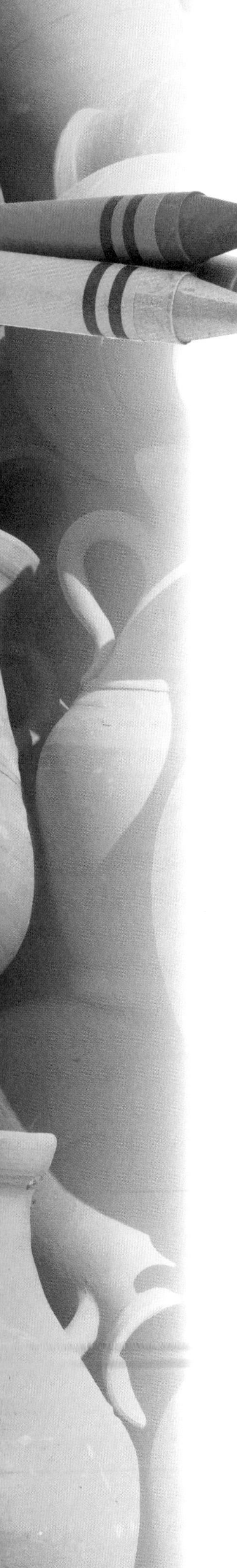

Directions

1. Give each child a coloring page. Instruct children to choose one color of crayon or marker, and that's all they'll color with until you give them instructions.
2. After a few moments, instruct children to exchange markers. Give specific instructions such as:
   - **Pass the crayon to the person on your right.**
   - **Pass the marker to the person across from you.**
   - **Pass the marker to someone wearing green.**
3. The last example means some kids won't have anything to color with, while others will have a choice. That's fine. But if you use instructions like that, you may want to follow them up with something like, **Put all the markers in the center of the table and choose a color you haven't used yet!**

Conversation

It was fun following the instructions, but I'll bet your picture didn't end up the way you thought it would at first. Sometimes life doesn't work out the way we planned. But if we talk to God every day and seek to follow his will, everything will work out just fine! Even if it is different than we expected.

Snack It!

Milk and Cookies

Materials

cups or boxes of milk (1 per child)

2–3 cookies per child

Overview

Children eat a typical midnight snack of milk and cookies to remember that God called Samuel in the middle of the night.

Conversation

Have you ever seen a cartoon character get up in the middle of the night wanting a snack? Or maybe you or someone in your family gets up around midnight wanting a snack? Milk and cookies end up being a top choice for midnight snacks! To remind us of Samuel getting up to listen to God in the middle of the night, we are having our own midnight snack of milk and cookies—right now!

Talk about It!

Basic Questions

1. Why was Hannah sad? *She did not have any children. She wanted a baby.*
2. Hannah wanted a child so badly that she promised God what? *That she would give the child back to God to serve him.*
3. Who trained Samuel? *Eli.*
4. Who was calling Samuel in the middle of the night? *God.*
5. What did God tell Samuel? *That he was going to punish Eli's family.*
6. When Samuel grew older, what did Israel want? *A king.*
7. Why did the Israelites want a king? *(1) Samuel's sons were not good judges; (2) all the other nations had one.*
8. How did Samuel know who God had picked as king? *God told him exactly where he'd find him. God told him who to pick.*
9. Who did God tell Samuel to anoint as the first king of Israel? *Saul.*

Go Further

1. What is it called when we talk to God and listen for his voice? *Prayer.*
2. How important is prayer and listening for God? (See Matthew 26:36–44.)
3. What are some things you could do today to start listening to God's voice and following him better?

Wrap It Up!

Refer to the time line.

Samuel was the last judge of the 300-year era of judges. Very early in life, Samuel heard God's voice and listened to him. The Lord was with Samuel as he led the Israelites until the time the people demanded a king. God revealed to Samuel that they were not rejecting him, but that the Israelites were actually rejecting God as their king. The era of the judges comes to an end as Samuel anointed the first king of Israel, Saul.

LESSON OVERVIEW

King Solomon began his reign as a wise king, but then he disobeyed God. God took most of the kingdom away from King Solomon. This chapter focuses on the Northern Kings of Israel and what it means to do right in the eyes of God.

1 Kings 3,11; 2 Kings 17

Israel's Kings

Time Line
931—722 B.C.

Key Events & People
Division of the Israelites; 19 Northern kings, King Solomon

Introduce It!

Time Line Materials needed. (See p. 4.)

Begin the lesson in prayer. Thank God for his wisdom and guidance.

Memory Verse

Jesus replied, "All who love me will do what I say. My Father will love them, and we will come and make our home with each of them. Anyone who doesn't love me will not obey me."

John 14:23–24

Whose idea was it for Israel to have a king? God's idea or the people's? Children respond. Having a human king was not best for God's people, nor was it what God wanted for them. God wanted to be their king, but he granted the people what they wanted. After the era of the judges (refer to time line at 1350 B.C.), God made Saul the first king of Israel. After Saul, God chose David as the next king.

David had HUGE faith in God. When he was young, he defeated a giant with a tiny slingshot and a prayer. He was such a great king that God promised him a lasting dynasty. David's son Solomon became the next king. Things get a little more complicated after King Solomon's reign, though. The kingdom gets split because of something King Solomon does. That's where we pick up today, in Israel at 931 B.C. Place time line marker at 931 B.C.

Tell It!

Choose a way to tell the story while reading the account from the Bible or telling it in your own words. Ideas for creative storytelling include acting it out, using props, or incorporating pictures.

The Wise King Solomon

King David was a GREAT king! He was referred to as a man after God's own heart. His son Solomon started his reign as a good king like his father!

One night, God appeared to King Solomon in a dream. He told King Solomon that he would give him anything he wanted. If God asked you this, what would you say? Children respond.

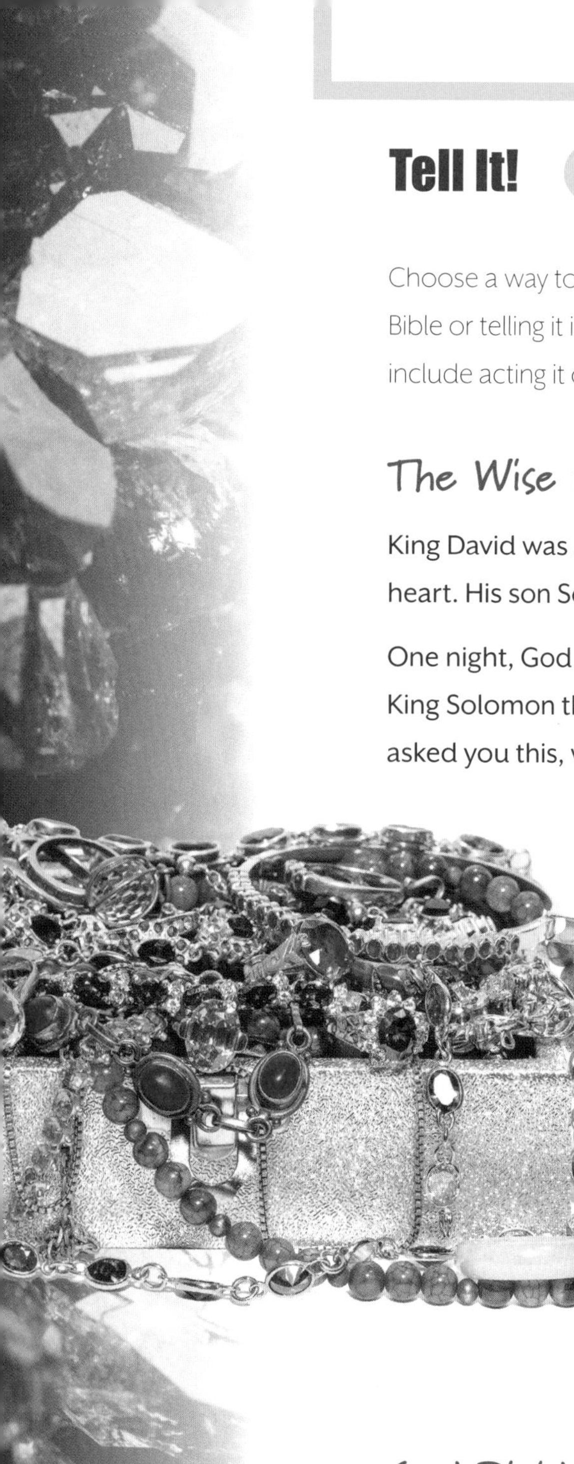

Those sound like some great requests. Now, King Solomon remembered how wise his father was. So he didn't ask for riches or power. He realized God had placed him in a very important position. He was the king of God's chosen people! And he had no idea what he was doing.

Read 1 Kings 3:7–9.

God was pleased with King Solomon's request. He gave King Solomon wisdom, just as he asked. But he also gave King Solomon what he didn't ask for. He gave him riches! He gave him fame! He was the best king in the world! As long as he obeyed God, God promised to give him a long life.

God Divides the Kingdom

King Solomon was wise for many years, but after a while he stopped listening to God. He married many women who did not believe in God. God had told King Solomon not to marry these women because they worshiped false gods. He did not listen to God and married them anyway. Even though King Solomon loved and followed God, he started building places of worship for his wives' fake gods. God was NOT happy with this.

Read 1 Kings 11:9–13.

Optional

Show children a map of the division of the Northern and Southern Kingdoms.

Because of King Solomon's sin, God split the kingdom into two kingdoms, the Northern Kingdom and the Southern Kingdom. The Northern Kingdom kept the name *Israel,* while the Southern Kingdom took the name *Judah.*

God had promised King David that someone from his line would be on the throne forever. So, instead of taking the whole kingdom away from King Solomon, God gave him two tribes to rule. The other ten tribes became part of the Northern Kingdom.

Through the prophet Ahijah, God picked a man named Jeroboam to rule the Northern Kingdom. God told Jeroboam that if he would follow him the way David did, he would give him an enduring dynasty. God also promised to be with him. Sadly, Jeroboam chose not to follow God.

The Northern Kings

Refer to time line.

The Northern Kingdom lasted from 931 B.C. – 722 B.C. During that 209-year period, Israel went through nineteen kings! And every one of them did evil in the eyes of the Lord. They did not follow God. God took the kingdom away from King Solomon for doing the same thing. Do you think God punished the Northern Kingdom? Children respond.

Read 2 Kings 17:18.

Just as God punished King Solomon for not following him, God punished the Northern Kingdom, too. The people of Israel (the Northern Kingdom) were taken from their homes and into exile in Assyria in 722 B.C. Refer to time line. Judah (the Southern Kingdom) still remained, but the Northern Kingdom ended because of its disobedience.

Pray It!

Dear Lord, there are so many decisions in life. Teach me to turn to you when I don't know which way to go. Thank you for always listening to me. In Jesus' name, amen.

Apply It!

Choose any of these activities for your lesson. Use more than one if time allows. For any of these activities, discuss the **Talk about It!** questions on page 108 as time allows.

Show It!

Good and Bad

Materials
poster board
sticky notes
markers

Overview

Children write down the qualities of good and bad kings on sticky notes and put them on a giant crown template.

Preparation

Draw a giant crown on poster board. Alternatively, draw a giant crown on a whiteboard. Draw a line down the center of the crown. On one side of the crown print *good*; on the other side of the crown print *bad*.

Directions

1. Hand out sticky notes to the children.
2. Children write a quality of a bad king on a sticky note and place it on the bad side of the crown.
3. Children write a quality of a good king on a sticky note and place it on the good side of the crown.
4. Talk about the qualities of good and bad rulers.

Conversation

Those are some great answers! What do you think would make the worst king ever in God's eyes? Children respond. **What do you think would make the best king ever in God's eyes?** Children respond.

Act It Out!

Nineteen Very Bad Kings

Materials
paper
pen
crown

Overview

Children take turns becoming a king of the Northern Kingdom, Israel.

Preparation

Before class, print each of the names of the northern kings on slips of paper, including the numerical order as well as the length of their reign on each slip. Place the crown on a chair set to one side of the activity area.

Kings of Israel, Northern Kingdom	Kings of Judah, Southern Kingdom
1. Jeroboam 1, 22 years	1. Rehoboam, 17 years
2. Nadab, 2 years	2. Abijam, 3 years
3. Baasha, 24 years	3. Asa, 41 years
4. Elah, 2 years	4. Jehoshaphat, 25 years
5. Zimri, 1 week	5. Jehoram, 8 years
6. Omri, 12 years	6. Ahaziah, 1 year
7. Ahab, 22 years	7. Athaliah (Queen), 6 years
8. Ahaziah, 2 years	8. Joash, 40 years
9. Jehoram (Joram), 12 years	9. Amaziah, 29 years
10. Jehu, 28 years	10. Azariah (Uzziah), 52 years
11. Jehoahaz, 17 years	11. Jotham, 16 years
12. Jehoash, 16 years	12. Ahaz, 16 years
13. Jeroboam 2, 41 years	13. Hezekiah, 29 years
14. Zachariah, 6 months	14. Manasseh, 55 years
15. Shallum, 1 month	15. Amon, 2 years
16. Menahem, 10 years	16. Josiah, 31 years
17. Pekhiah, 2 years	17. Jehoahaz, 3 months
18. Pekah, 20 years	18. Jehoiakim, 11 years
19. Hoshea, 9 years	19. Jehoiachin, 3 months
	20. Zedekiah, 11 years

Optional

If you have enough time with your kids, prepare slips that have the names, numbers, and reigns of the rulers of the Southern Kingdom, Judah. Remember that there were eight good kings of Judah—Asa, Jehoshaphat, Joash, Amaziah, Azariah, Jotham, Hezekiah, and Josiah. Have children cheer these kings instead of saying "Boo!"

Today we are going to pretend to be the nineteen different kings of the Northern Kingdom, Israel!

Directions

1. Distribute one slip with the number, name, and reign of one of the Northern Kingdom kings to each child. If you have fewer than nineteen children, you will need to give more than one slip to each child.
2. As you call out the number of each king, the child with that number comes forward, places the crown on their head and takes a seat on the "throne."
3. The child on the throne then reads the name and length of their reign. Because they were a bad king, have the remaining children call out, "Boo!" before you call out another number.
4. When you call another number, the child on the throne stands, places the crown back on the "throne," and returns to their seat. Play continues until all the kings have taken the throne.

Conversation

There were nineteen very bad kings in the Northern Kingdom. They served from one week to forty-one years. Imagine living in Israel at that time. Two hundred nine years of very bad kings, all who did evil in God's eyes. It couldn't have been an easy time for anyone!

Play It!

A Divided Kingdom

Overview

Children play a variation of freeze tag on two opposing teams to represent the divided kingdoms of Israel and Judah.

Directions

1. Divide the children into two groups, frozen and not frozen.
2. Select one child from each group to be *King* of their half. The goal is for the *Kings* to tag everyone to be in their kingdom, frozen or not frozen.
3. Whenever a child is tagged by a *King*, they are on that kingdom by either frozen or not frozen.
4. If a *King* succeeds in tagging everyone to their kingdom, they win.
5. Change *Kings* and continue playing as time allows.

Conversation

In our game, there were two kingdoms against each other. The Kings kept trying to get everyone on their kingdom's side. They wanted their kingdom to win.

We read about God dividing the Kingdom of Israel into two kingdoms. Do you think those two kingdoms fought against each other? Children respond. Yes! There were wars and fights between the Northern and Southern kingdoms. Just like in our game, each kingdom wanted to be the only kingdom!

Craft It!

Kingly Crowns

Overview

Children decorate crowns.

Preparation

Cut strips of cardstock or construction paper long enough to wrap around a child's head.

Materials

cardstock or construction paper, yellow or gold

scissors

tape

decorating supplies (sequins, stickers, etc.)

crayons or markers

Directions

1. Children decorate their crowns. Children write out the things they would do as king or queen on the crown.
2. Tape the edges of the crown so that it sits on the child's head.
3. Children share what they would do if they were king or queen.

Conversation

If you were king or queen, what would you do? Children respond. The kings of the Northern Kingdom could have done great things with God's support, but because they chose not to follow him, their kingdom fell. The Northern Kingdom was taken over by its enemies, and the people were forced to live in exile in Assyria. The Northern kings did not make the good choice to follow the Lord.

Snack It!

Dividing Grapes

Materials

paper or plastic cups

red and green grapes

Overview

Children separate grapes by color and then eat them.

Preparation

Place several of both kinds of grapes into cups, making one cup for each child.

Directions

1. Give each child a cup.
2. Look at the grapes in your cup. Did you know that grapes come in many different colors? They can be green, red, black, yellow, pink, or purple! They are all different colors, but they are still all grapes. For now, split your grapes so that all the red grapes are together and all the green grapes are together.
3. Children eat their grapes.

Conversation

The Israelites were split into kingdoms, but they were still Israelites, even though they were apart. Throughout history, the Israelites are split up and scattered, but when they turned to God, they were brought back together.

Talk about It!

Basic Questions

1. When God told King Solomon that he would give him anything he wanted, what did King Solomon ask for? *Wisdom.*
2. What was so bad about King Solomon having many wives? *They worshiped false gods. King Solomon built temples for those false gods.*
3. What punishment did King Solomon receive for building temples for his wives' false gods? *God took the kingdom away from him.*
4. What were the names of the two kingdoms after God split Israel in two? *The Northern Kingdom of Israel and the Southern Kingdom of Judah.*
5. Which half of the kingdom was ruled by King Solomon and David's line? *The Southern Kingdom of Judah.*
6. The Northern Kingdom had how many kings? *Nineteen kings.*
7. How many of the kings did right in the eyes of the Lord? *None.*
8. When God split the kingdom, who became the Northern Kingdom's king? *Jeroboam.*
9. Did Jeroboam follow the Lord and receive the blessing God promised? *No.*
10. In 722, the Northern Kingdom came to an end. What happened to the people? *They were taken into exile in Assyria.*

Go Further

1. The kings of Israel broke what commandment that God gave to Moses for his people? (See Exodus 20:3.)
2. Are there areas of your life where you are struggling to follow God? What does doing right in God's eyes look like in your life?

Wrap It Up!

God gave his people a king even though it was not what he wanted. King Solomon did not listen to God's commandments, so God split the kingdoms.

Refer to the time line.

From 931 – 722 B.C., all of the nineteen kings that ruled the Northern Kingdom disobeyed God. They did evil in the eyes of the Lord, and because of this, God punished his people. They were exiled in Assyria. God wants everyone to follow his commands and rules because he knows what is best for us. He created every single person, and he loves us dearly.

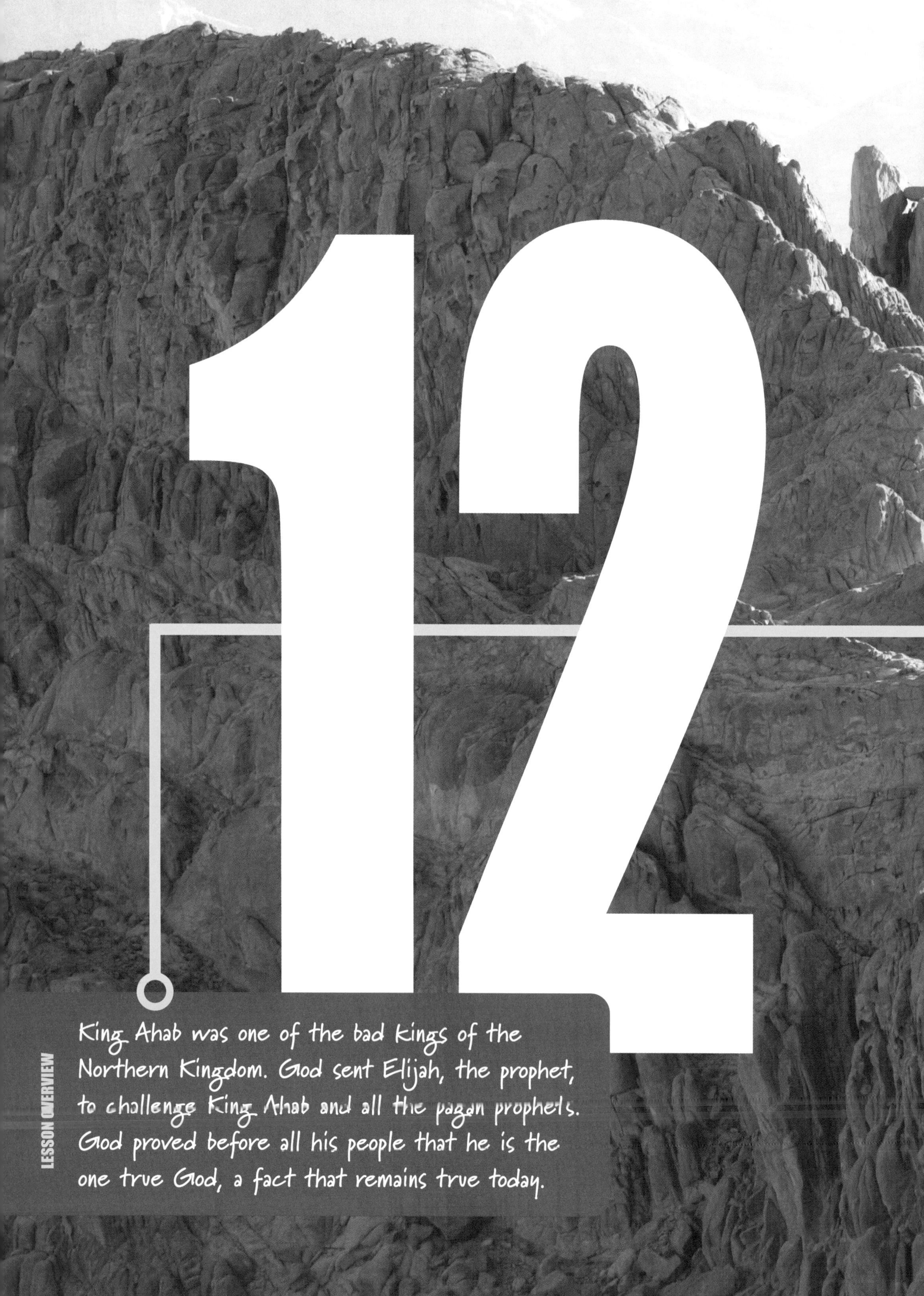
12
LESSON OVERVIEW
King Ahab was one of the bad kings of the Northern Kingdom. God sent Elijah, the prophet, to challenge King Ahab and all the pagan prophets. God proved before all his people that he is the one true God, a fact that remains true today.

1 Kings 16:29–18

Elijah on Mount Carmel

Introduce It!

Time Line

870 B.C. – 845 B.C.

Key Events & People

Challenge on Mount Carmel; Elijah, King Ahab

Memory Verse

All the world from east to west will know there is no other God. I am the LORD, and there is no other.

Isaiah 45:6

Time Line Materials needed. (See p. 4.)

Start today's lesson in prayer. Thank God for who he is and that he hears his people.

The Israelites had a divided kingdom. Over and over again, the kings of the Northern Kingdom of Israel did evil in the sight of the Lord. One of those kings was King Ahab. King Ahab was the seventh king of the Northern Kingdom, taking the throne around 874 B.C.

Place time line marker at 874 B.C.

God's Word tells us that King Ahab did more evil in the eyes of the Lord than any other king (1 Kings 16:30). King Ahab led the people of Israel in worshiping and building altars to the false god Baal. The people were deep in sin. During this time, however, God raised up a prophet named Elijah, who would show the people that our God is the true God.

Tell It!

Choose a way to tell the story while reading the account from the Bible or telling it in your own words. Ideas for creative storytelling include acting it out, using props, or incorporating pictures.

God Is Real

Let's say our memory verse. Children recite Isaiah 45:6. This verse tells us that God is the Lord, and there is no one like him. Have any of you ever met someone who did not believe that God is real? Children respond. Tell a personal story if age-appropriate and as time allows.

If someone came up to you and asked how you know God is real, what would you say? Children respond. The Bible gives many examples of people who proclaimed that God is real, including Elijah.

Elijah Was Fed by Ravens

Play the Raven Race found on page 115.

RAVEN RACE

God was upset with the Israelites again. Their king, Ahab, had built altars to other gods, and the people worshiped those false gods. God sent the prophet Elijah to King Ahab with a message.

Read 1 Kings 17:1.

Remember that Israel is a desert, and water is very important. So when Elijah told Ahab there was not going to be any water again until he gave the word, he just gave Ahab some really bad news! So he ran away from King Ahab.

God told Elijah to hide by a stream, and that the ravens would bring him food. And they did! Every morning and evening, ravens brought him bread and meat. God provided for Elijah during the drought. God provided for Elijah's needs in a way that only he could!

Contest on Mount Carmel

The famine lasted three years, and the land of Israel dried up. Animals were dying. People were dying. There was hardly any food or drink. King Ahab searched everywhere for Elijah, but he could not find him.

Then, God told Elijah to go to King Ahab again. This time, Elijah had more than a message for King Ahab. He had a challenge.

Read 1 Kings 18: 16–21.

Elijah wanted to prove to King Ahab that the Lord is God, and that King Ahab's god, Baal, was not real. Elijah and the prophets of Baal each built an altar. They put a sacrifice on top. Then Elijah told the prophets of Baal to call out to their god. "Pray that he sets the altar on fire," Elijah ordered. The prophets of Baal prayed all day long. They danced around the altar. They cut themselves. But nothing worked.

When it was evening, Elijah said it was his turn. He had the people pour water all over his altar. Then, he prayed.

Read 1 Kings 18: 36–39.

God sent fire from heaven so hot that it burned the wet wood and it burned up the water and even the rocks! There was no doubt in anyone's eyes that the Lord is God. After that, the rain came. The one true God provided for his people again.

Why didn't Baal send fire down on his offering? Children respond.
He isn't real! God showed that he alone is God.

Pray It!

Dear God, thank you for forgiving me every time I do something wrong. Over and over again, I put my faith in other people or other things. Help me to always focus on you. In Jesus' name, amen.

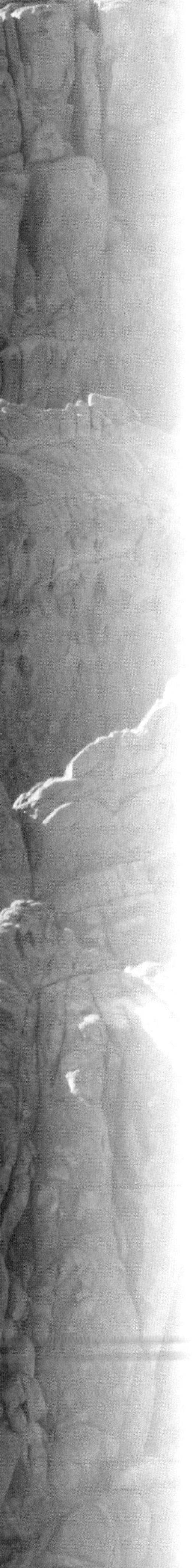

Apply It!

Choose any of these activities for your lesson. Use more than one if time allows. For any of these activities, discuss the **Talk about It!** questions on page 117 as time allows.

Show It!

Real or Not?

Materials
real rock(s)
fake rock(s)
rock candy
hammer

Overview

Children explore the differences between real and fake rocks and discuss how we can know that our God is the one true God.

In today's Bible story, we heard about fake gods and the one true God. Who did Elijah worship? Children respond. **That's right, the one true God. Today, we're going to talk about how to tell the difference between things that are fake and things that are real.**

Directions

1. Place real rock(s), fake rock(s), and rock candy where children can see them. Place hammer nearby.
2. Say, **Of these rocks, one or more may be real. The others are fake.** Ask a volunteer to come forward and identify a fake rock. **Are you sure it's fake? Why do you think it isn't real?** Volunteer explains.
3. Let's watch what happens when the rocks are hit with a hammer.
4. Choose another volunteer to test the rocks by tapping them with the hammer (no power swings!). **What happened to each rock?** (The real rock crumbled. The fake rock was rubbery and bounced. The rock candy shattered.)

Conversation

Sometimes you can tell what is fake just by looking at it. The color of the rock candy told you that it was fake. The fake rock looked like a real rock. But when it was hit with a hammer, we knew it was fake by what it did. We know that God is the one true God because of all the great things he has done. How did the events in our Bible story show that our God is the one true God and that Baal was a fake god? Children respond.

Act It Out!

Elijah's Altar

Materials

four chairs

empty water jugs

red, orange, and yellow tissue paper

Overview

Children act out setting up an altar like Elijah.

Today we are going to set up an altar just like Elijah. Let's work together.

Directions

1. Children work together to set up the chairs so that the seats face inward. This is the altar.
2. Children walk around the altar pretending to dig a ditch.
3. Children hold the empty water jugs over the altar and pretend to pour water all over it.
4. Children hold hands around the altar and shout, "Show yourself, true God!"
5. Place tissue paper on the altar to show it lit up!

Conversation

Elijah had a purpose for the competition on Mount Carmel. He asked God to answer his prayers and light the sacrifice with fire to show the people that he alone was God. Elijah wanted to turn the people's hearts back to the one true God!

Play It!

Raven Race

Materials

paper wads

laundry basket, 1 per team

Overview

Teams race to place pretend food in a basket, reminding them of how God sent ravens to give food to Elijah.

Preparation

Place paper wads in the middle of the playing area.

Directions

1. Divide the children into two to four teams.
2. Give each team an empty laundry basket.
3. Children will race to get the most food (paper wads) into their team's basket. They can only carry one piece at a time.
4. The team with the most food wins!

Conversation

How did God supply Elijah with food? Children respond. **God sent ravens with food. A false god like Baal couldn't have done that. Only the true God could have done it!**

Craft It!

Names of God Paper Chain

> **Materials**
>
> 1-inch wide strips of colored paper
>
> tape
>
> crayons or markers
>
> **Optional** Provide list with names of God for the children to use as a reference.

Overview

Children create a paper chain containing some of the names of God.

Directions

1. Children write one name of God on each strip of paper.
2. Tape together the ends of one strip to make the first link for the chain.
3. The first child to finish writing on a strip, loops it inside the first link and tapes it to make a second link.
4. Children repeat step three until all the strips are links.

Conversation

God has a lot of names! With all these names, just how many gods are there? Children respond. **There is only ONE God. God proved on Mount Carmel that he alone is God. As our memory verse this week reminds us, there is no one like the Lord our God!**

Snack It!

S'mores

> **Materials**
>
> paper plates
>
> plastic spoons
>
> graham-cracker squares
>
> chocolate squares
>
> marshmallow fluff

Overview

Children eat s'mores as a reminder of the fire God sent to Elijah's altar.

Directions

1. Give each child a paper plate and a plastic spoon.
2. Children sandwich a square of chocolate and a spoonful of marshmallow fluff between two graham-cracker squares.
3. Children eat their s'mores.

Conversation

Have you ever eaten s'mores around a campfire? Children respond. **Our snack reminds us of the fire God sent to light Elijah's altar. What was special about the fire God sent?** Children respond. **It was so hot that it burned up the wet wood and even the water and the rocks!**

Talk about It!

Basic Questions

1. Which kingdom had only kings who did not follow the Lord? *The Northern Kingdom.*
2. Which king did the most evil in the eyes of the Lord? *King Ahab.*
3. What was Elijah's first message to King Ahab? *Because of King Ahab's disobedience, there would be no rain until Elijah said so.*
4. How did God provide for Elijah? *He sent food by ravens and provided water from a brook.*
5. How long did the drought last? *Three years.*
6. What was Elijah's second message to King Ahab? *A challenge at Mount Carmel to see who was the true God.*
7. What false god did King Ahab worship? *Baal.*
8. What happened when the prophets called upon Baal to light fire to their offering? *Nothing.*
9. What unusual thing did Elijah do when he set up his offering? *He dumped jugs of water on the altar.*
10. What happened when God set Elijah's altar on fire? *It burned the wet wood, the sacrifice, the water, and the rocks. Then, the people declared that Elijah's God was real.*

Go Further

1. God answered Elijah's prayer with a fire so hot that it burned up the rocks. How does God answer the prayers of his people today? *(Jeremiah 29:12)*
2. How would you tell someone today that God is real and that he is the one true God?

Wrap It Up!

Refer to the time line.

Under King Ahab's reign, the people in the Northern Kingdom of Israel worshiped the false god Baal. The prophet Elijah showed the people not only that Baal was not real, but also how powerful the one true God is! After the competition on Mount Carmel, all of the people knew that the Lord alone is God!

MISCELLANEOUS

Books

13
LESSON OVERVIEW
The prophet Jonah disobeyed God when he was told to go to Nineveh. Jonah was swallowed by a big fish and prayed for redemption. God was merciful and gave Jonah a second chance. Children will learn the importance of prayer and mercy.

Jonah 1–4

Jonah

Introduce It!

Time Line

781 B.C.

Key Events & People

Jonah swallowed by a fish; Jonah, Ninevites

Memory Verse

Listen closely to my prayer, O Lord; hear my urgent cry.

Psalm 86:6

Time Line Materials needed. (See p. 4.)

Begin the lesson in prayer. Thank God for his mercy and his desire to guide us always.

The nation of Israel was still divided because of King Solomon's disobedience. The people from both the Northern and Southern Kingdoms were stuck in a cycle similar to the one during the era of the judges. Lead children to do motions they learned as you review the Cycle of Apostasy:

1. The Israelites forgot about God.
2. They were punished because of their disobedience.
3. They cried out to God for help.
4. God sent a prophet to lead the people back to him.

During the reign of King Jeroboam II from the Northern Kingdom of Israel, there was a prophet named Jonah. Jonah lived around 781 B.C. Place time line marker at 781 B.C. Jonah is one of the most famous prophets, and today we will find out why.

Tell It!

Choose a way to tell the story while reading the account from the Bible or telling it in your own words. Ideas for creative storytelling include acting it out, using props, or incorporating pictures.

A Job for Jonah

God had an important job for Jonah and told him exactly what he wanted him to do. Let's read and see if Jonah did what God told him to do or if Jonah chose to disobey.

Read Jonah 1:1–3.

God had a message for Jonah to deliver to the people of Nineveh, but he did not do what God said. Nineveh was the capital of the Assyrian empire. It was HUGE. It took three whole days to see the whole city, and it had 120,000 people living there (Jonah 3:3, 4:11). Jonah knew that wicked and powerful people lived there. He was scared. He didn't want to tell them that God would destroy their city. So instead of listening to God, he went in the opposite direction. He boarded a ship headed to Tarsus.

Simon Says

Start the lesson by playing Simon Says.

What do you have to do to win Simon Says? Children respond. You have to do exactly what Simon says, not what you see. Did you know that the rules of Simon Says work great for following God, too? We should do exactly what God says!

Swallowed by a Fish

Read Jonah 1:4–17.

When Jonah got on board, he went to sleep. God was angry with Jonah's disobedience, so he sent a violet storm. It rocked the boat back and forth so hard that the sailors thought the ship would break in half.

Jonah knew the storm was because of his disobedience, so he told the men to toss him into the sea so the storm would stop. The storm stopped just like Jonah thought, and then God sent a big fish to swallow Jonah!

Is it possible for a human being to be swallowed by a big fish? Believe it or not, it is very possible. There are certain whales with no teeth. They could swallow a person whole without hurting them. It might seem really scary to be swallowed by a fish, but it was God's mercy. Inside the fish, Jonah prayed and prayed. Then, God gave Jonah a second chance. The fish spat him out, and Jonah went to Nineveh.

Nineveh Was Saved

When Jonah arrived in Nineveh, he told the people that they had forty days until God would destroy their city. Do you think the people believed Jonah? Children respond.

The people did believe Jonah. The King of Nineveh told everyone to fast and pray. Even the animals were not allowed to eat. He thought if everyone in the HUGE city prayed, then maybe God would change his mind. The King was right. God saw that the people of Nineveh stopped living violently and truly said they were sorry. God did not destroy the city.

Do you think Jonah was happy about this news? Children respond. No! Jonah was mad when he heard that God would not destroy Nineveh. "Remember how bad those people were?" Jonah argued. "Remember how many evil things they did? How can you just forgive them?" Jonah could not believe how merciful God was.

Read what God said to Jonah in Jonah 4:11.

God is merciful to anyone who says that they are sorry. He is always there to listen, and he will always forgive.

Pray It!

Dear God, thank you for always accepting me as I am. Even when I do something wrong, you are always merciful. Help me to be merciful like you. Teach me to be slow to anger and quick to forgive. In Jesus' name, amen.

Apply It!

Choose any of these activities for your lesson. Use more than one if time allows. For any of these activities, discuss the **Talk about It!** questions on page 127 as time allows.

Show It!

Pray Every Day

Materials
- flashlight with batteries
- potted plant
- votive candle
- match or lighter
- large, wide-mouthed jar

Overview

Children explore what different objects need in order to work. Discuss how we need to talk with God every day in order to live the very best lives.

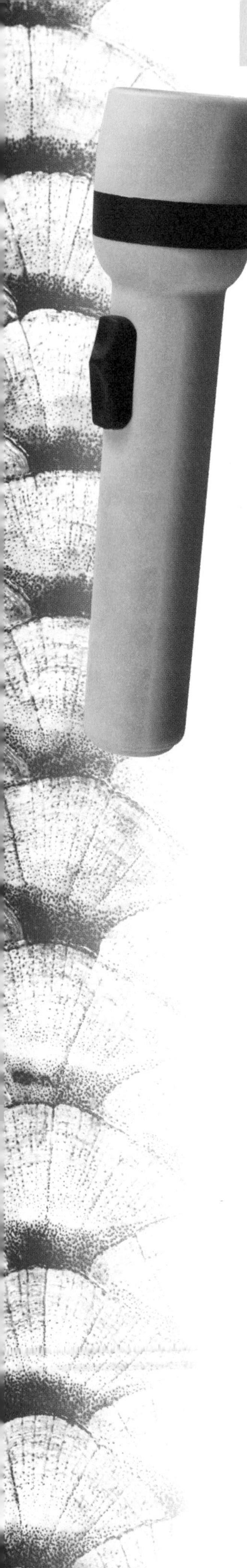

In today's Bible story, Jonah prayed to God for help. Asking for help is one reason to pray to God. But there are many others! When we pray to God every day, we get to know him better and love him more. Knowing God and his will for our lives helps us live the very best life. Let's look at some objects and discuss what they need in order to work.

Directions

1. Show children the flashlight. **What does this flashlight need in order to work?** *Working batteries, a bulb.* **What else needs batteries to work?**
2. Show the potted plant. **What does this plant need to live?** *Soil, sunlight, water.* **What else needs water and sunlight to grow?**
3. Show children the candle and use match or lighter to light it. **What does fire need to make a flame?** *Fuel, oxygen.* Cover the candle with the jar and watch what happens when the fire runs out of oxygen. **What else needs oxygen?**
4. **What are some things you need to live?** *Food, shelter, water, air, etc.*

Conversation

We've talked about what we need to live and what these different objects need to do what they are intended to do. In order for us to live the best life that God has planned for us, we need to talk to him every day. What is something you'd like to talk to God about right now? Let's take a few moments for silent prayer. Allow a few moments for children to pray silently, and then close by praying aloud.

Act It Out!

Materials

construction paper
marker
masking tape
2 sailor hats
2 swim rings
2 stick ponies

Jonah Sequence Relay

Overview

In teams, children will relay through the account of Jonah.

Preparation

On separate sheets of construction paper, draw the numerals 1, 2, 3, and 4. Make two sets.

Use masking tape to make a start line. Create a path for each team by placing each #1 sheet on the ground, several feet from the start line. Place a sailor hat on each #1. Several feet from #1, place the sheets with #2 and a swim ring. Repeat for sheets with #3 (no object) and finally sheets with #4 and the stick ponies.

Directions

1. Divide children into two evenly numbered teams that line up behind the start line.
2. Demonstrate how to run the relay, by going to each spot in turn, and performing the action list at right.
3. At each spot, children will perform the motion and say the phrase.
4. The first player on each team runs to spot #1, says the appropriate line, performs the appropriate action, and then races to the next spot. Players continue racing to spots and doing the action until they have completed each action. Be prepared to remind players what the words and actions are.
5. When finished with all four stations, players return to their teams and tag the next player who completes the race.
6. The first team to complete the race answers one of the **Talk about It!** questions on page 127 or repeats the memory verse.

Spot 1

Say: "All aboard!"

Motion: Put on saior hat & motion to come.

Spot 2

Say: "Man overboard."

Motion: Put on the swim ring.

Spot 3

Say: "I'm sorry."

Motion: Kneel to pray.

Spot 4

Say: "To Nineveh!"

Motion: Gallop on the stick pony.

Conversation

God told Jonah to go to Nineveh, but Jonah did not obey. He ran away from God by boarding a ship headed to another city. When the storm came, Jonah was tossed overboard because he was running from God. He was swallowed by a big fish. Then, for three days, Jonah prayed to God and repented for not obeying him. After Jonah was spat out by the fish, God told him to go to Nineveh a second time. This time, Jonah obeyed!

Play It!

Fishy Fishy Cross My Ocean

Overview

Children race across a playing area and try not to get tagged by the Big Fish.

Directions

1. Choose one child to be the Big Fish. All other players are regular fish.
2. Play starts when Big Fish says, "Fishy, fishy, cross my ocean."
3. Players race across the playing area, trying to avoid the Big Fish. If a player is tagged, they become Seaweed. The Seaweed sit down exactly where they are tagged. As other players run by, they can tag them, but they cannot move from their spot.
4. The last untagged fish answers, or chooses a volunteer to answer, one of the **Talk about It!** questions. Player then becomes the Big Fish for the next round.
5. Continue playing as time and interest allow.

Conversation

The Big Fish did a great job tagging the little fish in our game. What happened to Jonah with a big fish? Children respond. Jonah was swallowed by a big fish because of his disobedience to God.

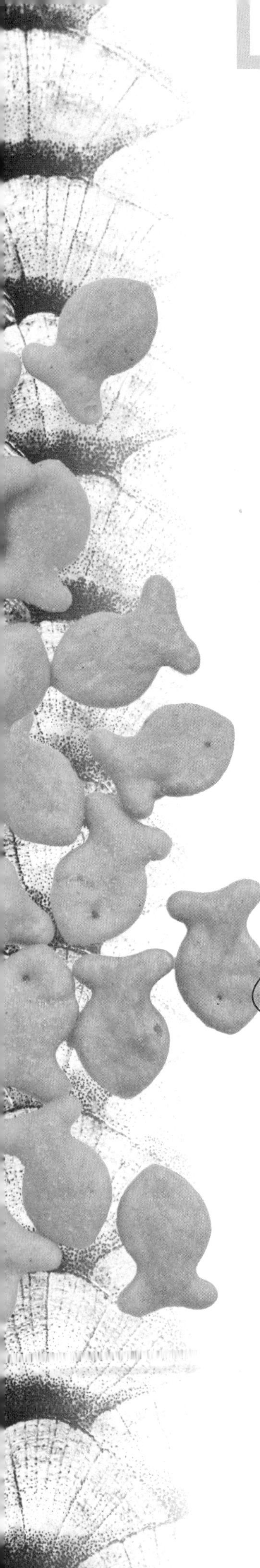

Craft It!

Prayer Jar

Materials

empty tin cans (1 per child)

duct tape

scissors

decorative tape or cardstock

markers

stickers

wooden craft sticks

Overview

Children make prayer jars.

Preparation

Cover the rim of the tin can with duct tape, covering any sharp edges.

Directions

1. Children decorate their tin cans with a few different options:
   - Wrap decorative tape around the can
   - Wrap and tape cardstock around the can; decorate with stickers and markers.
2. Children write prayer requests on craft sticks and place them in the cans.

Conversation

When Jonah was inside of the fish, what did he do? Children respond. **He knew he disobeyed God, so he repented. Are we only supposed to pray when things go bad in life, like being swallowed by a fish?** Children respond. **No! 1 Thessalonians 5:17 tells us that we are supposed to pray all the time. Your prayer jars can help you pray at home all of the time!**

Snack It!

Fish and Chips

Materials

fish-shaped crackers

potato chips

paper or plastic cups

Overview

Children eat fish-shaped crackers and potato chips to remember that Jonah was inside a big fish.

Directions

Children scoop fish-shaped crackers and potato chips into cups, and eat their snack.

Conversation

Jonah disobeyed God. God told Jonah to go to the people of Nineveh and deliver a message for them, but Jonah did not want to. God punishes disobedience. Our "fish and chips" snack today reminds us of Jonah's punishment, being in the belly of a fish for three whole days.

Talk about It!

Basic Questions

1. What did God want Jonah to do? *Take a message to Nineveh.*
2. How did Jonah disobey? *He boarded a ship headed to Tarsus (the opposite direction).*
3. On the way to Tarsus, what happened? *A storm came.*
4. Why did the storm stop? *Jonah was thrown into the sea.*
5. What happened to Jonah once he was thrown in the sea? *He was swallowed by a big fish.*
6. How long was Jonah inside the fish? *Three days.*
7. What did Jonah do inside the fish? *He prayed. He asked God to forgive him.*
8. What happened to Jonah after three days inside the fish? *God commanded the fish to spit Jonah out onto dry land.*
9. When God told Jonah a second time to go to Nineveh, what did Jonah do? *He obeyed.*
10. How did the people of Nineveh react to Jonah's news? *They fasted and prayed.*
11. How did Jonah react when the people of Nineveh changed their ways? *He was angry that they were not destroyed because they used to do bad things.*
12. Why did God not destroy Nineveh? *The people repented, and God is merciful.*

Go Further

1. What does it mean to be merciful?
2. Share a time that you were merciful to someone or a time that someone was merciful to you. How did it make you feel?
3. What does the Bible say about our prayers to God? (See 1 John 5:14–15.)

Wrap It Up!

God punished Jonah's disobedience with a violent storm. But, God showed mercy on him and sent a big fish to swallow Jonah. Inside the fish, Jonah repented through prayer. God was merciful to Jonah and gave him another chance to take the message to Nineveh. After three days inside the fish, God commanded it to spit Jonah out onto dry land. This time, when God commanded Jonah to take his message to Nineveh, Jonah obeyed. God punishes our disobedience, but he also gives us mercy!

14
LESSON OVERVIEW
Jerusalem is destroyed by Babylon and King Nebuchadnezzar. Judah's disobedience is punished. While learning about these events, the children will see that God is just, righteous, and merciful.

2 Kings 23:26–27,25:1–6; Jeremiah 25:5–8

Jerusalem Destroyed

Introduce It!

Time Line

586 B.C.

Key Events & People

Destruction of the Temple; Jeremiah, King Nebuchadnezzar, kings of Israel and Judah

Memory Verse

He will judge the world with justice and rule the nations with fairness.

Psalm 9:8

Time Line Materials needed. (See p. 4.)

Begin the lesson in prayer, thanking God for his justness and mercy.

The Kingdom of Israel was divided in two because of King Solomon's disobedience in 931 B.C. Refer to time line. Can anyone remember what King Solomon did to disobey the Lord? Children respond. King Solomon allowed temples to be built to worship the gods of his many wives.

After the division of the Kingdom in 931 B.C., there were nineteen kings and one queen who ruled over the Southern Kingdom of Judah. Some of these rulers were good and followed the Lord, but others did evil in the eyes of the Lord. Their punishment was the destruction of Jerusalem in 586 B.C. Place time line marker at 586 B.C.

King Solomon had built God's temple in Jerusalem. Today, we will discover what happened to this important city.

Tell It!

Choose a way to tell the story while reading the account from the Bible or telling it in your own words. Ideas for creative storytelling include acting it out, using props, or incorporating pictures.

The Kingdoms Did Evil

Do you do anything special on your birthday? Children respond. **It's nice to have a whole day dedicated to you. Now, imagine that on your birthday, your whole family decided to celebrate someone else—a pretend person. How would you feel?** Children respond.

You would be upset. In the same way, God's children stopped celebrating his goodness. They turned to other false gods. This made God burn with anger. Let me see your best angry face. Children respond.

The Israelites were already divided into two kingdoms, but now God scattered them. The Northern Kingdom of Israel was the first to be punished. Israel was attacked by Assyria and taken into exile in Assyria in 722 B.C. Refer to the time line.

Let me see your sad face. Children respond. **Judah, the Southern Kingdom, was still left. Some of the kings followed God. King Hezekiah was very good, and he destroyed many false temples. Let me hear your cheers!** Children respond. **King Josiah began to restore God's temple, and he found an ancient scroll. After reading it, he removed the false temples just as God said to do. Let me hear your cheers!** Children respond.

Even though Judah had some good kings, most of them were bad. God decided to punish them, too.

Read 2 Kings 23:26–27.

What did God do to Jerusalem? Children respond. **He removed Judah, just like he did to Israel. The temple was destroyed, and the people were punished. Let me see your sad face.** Children respond.

The Temple Was Destroyed

Now, there was an enemy king who wanted the land of Israel. His name was King Nebuchadnezzar, and he was the King of Babylon. Whenever I say *Nebuchadnezzar* or *Babylon*, make an angry face and say, "Boo!" Let's practice. Children respond.

During the reign of King Jehoiakim of Judah, Nebuchadnezzar, King of Babylon, invaded the land. Jehoiakim worked with Nebuchadnezzar for three years until he rebelled. Jehoiakim's rebellion didn't go well for Judah. Nebuchadnezzar wanted control of the land, so he punished those that fought against him.

Read 2 Kings 25:1–6.

Nebuchadnezzar surrounded the city of Jerusalem with his soldiers from Babylon. No one could get in or out of the city because there were so many Babylonian soldiers. Judah surrendered to Nebuchadnezzar. Jehoiakim died, and the temple treasures were taken.

The Fall of Jerusalem

Play Jerusalem Falls found on page 132.

JERUSALEM FALLS

After Nebuchadnezzar captured Judah for Babylon, he made Zedekiah Judah's new king. Just like Jehoiakim before him, Zedekiah tried to rebel against Babylon, too. This made Nebuchadnezzar angry. What do you think happened? Children respond.

Babylon's army marched to Jerusalem to overtake the city. Let's all stand and march in place. Children respond. They broke through the wall surrounding Jerusalem. They invaded God's temple. They took everything, large and small, from the temple. All the gold, the cloths, the ceremonial items—everything. Whatever the Babylonians didn't take, they burned.

Let's sit and flutter our fingers like fire. Children respond.

Babylon destroyed the city of Jerusalem under King Zedekiah. The people were taken captive. They became servants to the Babylonians.

Why did God let this happen? Children respond. The people would not take God's warnings and turn to him. The prophet Jeremiah had warned over and over again what would happen if the people didn't turn back to God.

Read Jeremiah 25:5–8.

Did the people get only one warning to turn from their evil ways? Children respond. No! They were warned over and over to turn back to the Lord. Because of their disobedience, they were punished. For seventy years, the Israelites lived in exile.

Pray It!

Dear God, please teach me to hear your words. It's hard to listen to you sometimes. Help me to follow your teachings. In Jesus' name, amen.

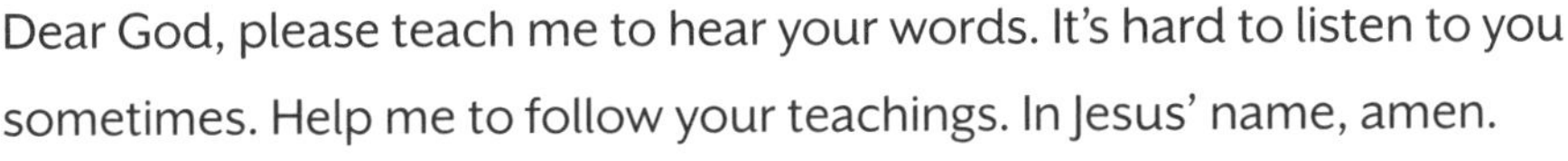

Apply It!

Choose any of these activities for your lesson. Use more than one if time allows. For any of these activities, discuss the **Talk about It!** questions on page 135 as time allows.

Show It!

Stick with It

Overview

Children try out actions that are easy at first but become harder over time.

Let's all do some actions that may seem easy at first. But watch what happens the longer you keep going.

Directions

1. Ask a couple of volunteers to jog in place. Remind them to keep jogging as you lead other volunteers to do other actions:
    - Hold arms straight out to the side, parallel to the floor. Keep them up.
    - Hold your breath.
    - Hold a plank position.
    - Hop on one foot
2. Allow joggers to stop jogging. Ask all volunteers how they felt when they started, how they felt when they had to keep going, and how it felt to stop.

Conversation

All of these actions started off easy to do but got harder and harder over time. It can be that way with obeying Jesus, too. We might get excited about following Jesus on ~~Sunday when we come to church~~, but as the week goes on, it can be harder and harder to keep obeying. Remember, God will always give us the help we need to stick it out and keep obeying. All we have to do is ask!

Act It Out!

Jerusalem Falls

Materials
cardboard boxes

Overview

Teams create walls to protect treasure. Then, teams try to knock over the opposing team's wall and gain the treasure.

Directions

1. Divide the children into two groups: the Israelites and the Babylonians.
2. Each team works together to build a wall out of the cardboard boxes.
3. The children playing the Babylonians will break down the wall of Jerusalem and march the Israelites past their wall to captivity in Babylon.
4. Rebuild the wall and allow children to switch sides if time allows.

Conversation

What happened to Jerusalem and the people of Israel? Children respond. **Jerusalem was destroyed, and the people were taken into captivity for 70 years!**

Play It!

King of the Circle

> **Materials**
> soft ball that bounces, one for every 8–10 players.

Overview

Children pass a ball around a circle trying to move into the King's spot.

Directions

1. Children form circles with 8–10 players. Select one to be the King.
2. King starts off with the ball and bounce-passes it to another player.
3. The player bounce-passes it back to the King. If the player misses their pass, they move to the spot directly to the King's left.
4. If the King misses his pass, the player to their right becomes the King.

Conversation

Did you like it when another King took your spot? Children respond. **No way! Imagine how the Kings of Judah felt when the King of Babylon came and took over their land! This was the punishment for their disobedience and refusal to follow God.**

Craft It!

Mercy Mosaics

> **Materials**
> clear Con Tact paper
> ruler
> scissors
> colored tissue paper
> paper
> markers
> masking tape

Overview

Children make a mosaic cross as a reminder that Jesus saves us from sin.

Preparation

1. Cut Con-Tact paper into 8.5x11-inch rectangles, making two for each child.
2. Cut out approximately 1-inch tissue-paper squares, making dozens of each color. Tip: Use a paper cutter to make this easy.

Directions

1. Children draw a cross outline on their papers, filling as much of the page as possible. Children tape outline on table.
2. Children tape one rectangle of Con-Tact paper over the taped cross.
3. Children place tissue-paper squares on the Con-Tact paper, using the cross outline as a guide.
4. Children place a second piece of Con-Tact paper on top, sticky sides together. Press down.
5. Children cut out the crosses.

Conversation

Does anyone know why we made a cross today? Children respond. **We learned about God punishing Judah for the people's disobedience. God is righteous and just, so he must punish sin. He punishes our sin, too, but God showed mercy on us. He sent Jesus to die on the cross to save us from the punishment of sin.**

Snack It!

Chocolate Coins

Materials

chocolate coins, several per child

Overview

Chocolate coins remind us of King Nebuchadnezzar taking the treasure from God's temple.

Conversation

When King Nebuchadnezzar took over Jerusalem, he even took the treasure out of God's temple! What was the purpose of that treasure in the temple? It was honoring God. Why don't we have a temple today for God? Now, when we become members of God's family, he is always with us.

Talk about It!

Basic Questions

1. Why was the kingdom divided? *Because of King Solomon's disobedience.*
2. Which country invaded the Northern Kingdom of Israel? *Assyria.*
3. Which country invaded the Southern Kingdom of Judah? *Babylon.*
4. In which kingdom, the Northern or Southern, was Jerusalem located? *Southern.*
5. Were the Kings of Judah good or bad? *Some were good, but most were bad.*
6. Who was king of Babylon? *King Nebuchadnezzar.*
7. What prophet warned the people to turn back to God? *Jeremiah.*
8. What happened to the temple? *Its treasures were taken, and it was destroyed.*
9. What happened to the people of Jerusalem? *There were taken into exile.*
10. How long was the exile to last? *70 years.*

Go Further

1. What is mercy? *Mercy is giving you something you don't deserve.*
2. How did God show his mercy to the people of Judah?
   They were only in exile for seventy years.
3. How does God show mercy to us? (See Romans 6:23, John 3:16, Romans 5:8.)

Wrap It Up!

Refer to the time line.

Jerusalem was destroyed in 586 B.C., and God's people were punished for their disobedience. The prophet Jeremiah warned the people over and over to turn back to God, but they did not listen. Because God is just and must punish sin, Israel was punished for their disobedience. Jerusalem was destroyed, and the people were sent into exile for seventy years. Though God is just, he is also merciful. He was still working to fulfill his plan for Israel, even through their punishment!

15
LESSON OVERVIEW
God was silent for 400 years between the Old and New Testaments. Children will see that though God was silent, he was still working to fulfill his plan for humanity.

Luke 3:23–38; Hebrews 9:28

Years between Testaments

Introduce It!

Time Line
400 B.C.

Key Events & People
God is silent; ancestors of Jesus

Memory Verse
I tell you the truth, unless you are born again, you cannot see the Kingdom of God.
John 3:3

Time Line Materials needed. (See p. 4.)

Begin the lesson in prayer. Have children take turns talking to God in prayer. Remind the children that God always hears our prayers.

At the end of the Old Testament, God partially restored the people of Israel back to their land. After their exile in Babylon, small groups of Israelites began living in Jerusalem again. The prophets at the end of the Old Testament (like Nehemiah and Malachi) ministered to the Jews back in their homeland.

Place time line marker at 400 B.C. This takes us to 400 B.C., the end of the Old Testament and the time period between the testaments.

Tell It!

Choose a way to tell the story while reading the account from the Bible or telling it in your own words. Ideas for creative storytelling include acting it out, using props, or incorporating pictures.

The Theme of the Bible

Which books or TV series do you get excited about? Children respond. **Those are some good books and TV shows! Now imagine that after the first few books or episodes, you had to wait a long time for the next one to come out. Would it be hard to wait?** Children respond. **I bet it would be hard.**

The Bible is like a very long book series. The Old Testament is made up of thirty-nine books. Select seven volunteers and ask them to stand up. **OK, all my volunteers, hold up your hands, let me see your fingers, and let's count thirty-nine fingers.** Count off by ten on the volunteers' hands. Ask the fourth child to put down one finger.

Now, the Old Testament is the first book series. The second book series is the New Testament. This series has twenty-seven books. Let's count some more. Count fingers by tens. Ask the last child to put down three fingers.

Point to the seven volunteers with their hands up. **See how many books are in the Bible! And guess what, there were 400 years between the Old Testament and the New Testament. Can you imagine waiting 400 years for a new book or TV series?** Children respond. Volunteers put their hands down and sit down.

What happened in those 400 years between the testaments? God was silent. He did not send any more prophets to lead his people. If God was silent, does that mean that things weren't happening? Children respond. **No, God was still working to fulfill his plan for humanity, even when he was silent.**

The Old Testament tells us about our sin and points to the need for a Savior. There are prophecies all throughout the Old Testament pointing toward the Savior. Read Hebrews 9:28. **The New Testament is the fulfillment of that promise. God provides the way for our sins to be forgiven through Jesus Christ.**

Ancestors of Jesus Christ

The New Testament begins with the four gospels. The gospels of Matthew and Luke remind us of Jesus' ancestors and the promises that God made to them (Luke 3:23–38).

Refer to the time line. Then follow the list below. Ask the children to recall what each person is famous for and what God promised them:

- 4000 B.C., Adam: The first man, told to name all the animals, banned from the Garden of Eden.
- 4000 B.C., Eve: The first woman, the first to sin, banned from the Garden of Eden.
- 2344 B.C., Noah: Obeyed God and built an ark to survive the flood. God promised he would never flood the earth again.
- 2166 B.C., Abraham: God promised to make him into a great nation. He was told to sacrifice Isaac as a test.
- 2066 B.C., Isaac: Abraham's promised firstborn son.
- 1406 B.C., Rahab: Hid the Israelite spies from the King of Jericho and helped them escape.
- 1011 B.C., David: The second king of the United Kingdom, he fought a giant and God promised him a lasting dynasty.
- 971 B.C., Solomon: The third and final king of the United Kingdom, he asked God for wisdom and God gave him much more. Because he built temples to his wives' false gods, God split the kingdom of Israel.

These are just a few of the many earthly ancestors that the Bible lists in Jesus' genealogy. (See Matthew 1:1–17.) As we can see, God always keeps his promises.

Pray It!

Dear God, thank you for always keeping your promises. Help me to also keep my promises. Teach me to say what I mean always. In Jesus' name, amen.

Apply It!

Choose any of these activities for your lesson. Use more than one if time allows. For any of these activities, discuss the **Talk about It!** questions on page 143 as time allows.

Show It!

Silence from God

Overview

Leader demonstrates silence by not saying anything for one minute.

Directions

Stand in front of the children in complete silence for 1–2 minutes. Give the children time to feel very uncomfortable with the silence, but don't talk or answer any of their questions.

Conversation

How did you feel about that time of silence we just had? Children respond. Did you feel like you were being punished, maybe? Without instruction, you didn't know what you were supposed to be doing, did you?

Our moment of silence only lasted a couple of minutes. Could you imagine a moment of silence from God? Only instead of a few minutes of silence from God, imagine 400 years of silence. That's a very long time.

Act It Out!

Silent and Still

Overview

Children strike a pose and remain still for as long as possible.

Directions

1. Whisper a pose to a child. Some ideas include:
   - Hands in the air.
   - Stand on one leg.
   - Squat like a frog.
2. Like the game telephone, that child will whisper the pose to the person next to them. Whispering continues around the circle.
3. Children stand up and strike the pose they heard.
4. Children will remain silent and still for as long as they can.
5. See who can stay still and silent the longest.

Conversation

It can be hard to be silent and still. A couple of minutes being silent can seem like an eternity. Imagine not hearing from God for 400 years! God was silent, but he wasn't still! God was working for the good of his people during that period.

Play It!

A–Z Memory Game

Overview

Children try to remember items in alphabetical order.

Directions

1. Children sit in a circle or in a line.
2. First player says an item that starts with *A*.
3. Second player repeats the *A* item and then says an item that starts with *B*.
4. Play continues through the alphabet.

Conversation

Did you ever forget items in our game? Children respond. **Sometimes it's hard to remember lots of things. During the 400 years between the Old and New Testaments, did God forget about his people?** Children respond. **No! God never forgot about his people. He was working to accomplish his plan for them, even though he was silent.**

Craft It!

Bible Bookmarks

Overview

Children will create a bookmark.

We've covered many books of the Old Testament so far. Today, we'll make bookmarks to remind us of God's promises.

Preparation

Cut cardstock into strips (at least one per child).

Materials

cardstock

scissors

crayons and markers

Optional: decorating supplies

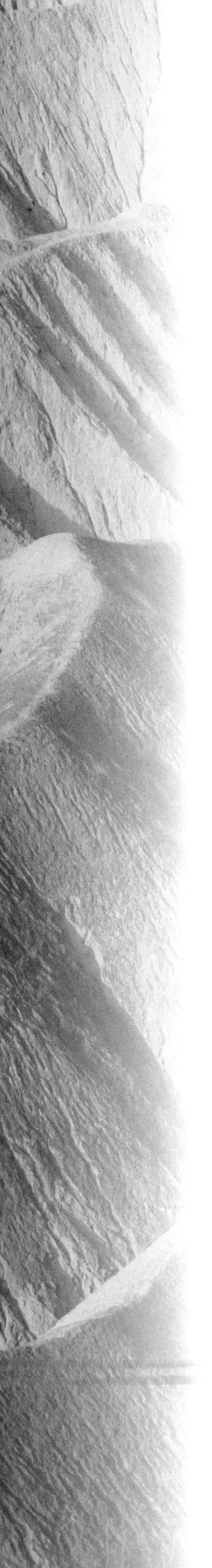

Directions

Children decorate their bookmarks. Here are some ideas:

- Write the name of your favorite Bible character from the Old Testament. Then, decorate the bookmark with things that remind you of them.
- Write the memory verse on your bookmark.
- Write the name of your favorite book of the Old Testament.
- Draw a picture of your favorite story.

Conversation

Both the Old and the New Testaments tell us of our need for a savior and the fulfillment of that promise! Your bookmarks can help hold your place as you read and learn what God's Word says!

Snack It!

Snacky Bookends

Overview

Children create bookends with their snacks.

Materials

crackers
cheese squares
paper plates

Directions

Children stand up their crackers and place a cheese square in between.

Conversation

You just made edible book ends! There are many books in the Old Testament and many books in the New Testament. But each book is part of the same story of our salvation.

Talk about It!

Basic Questions

1. Where did some of the Jews go at the end of the Old Testament, after the exile in Babylon? *They returned to Jerusalem.*
2. How many years was God silent? *400 years.*
3. The Old Testament tells us of our need for what? *A savior.*
4. Why do we need a Savior? *To save us from the punishment our sin. To become members of God's family.*
5. The New Testament tells the fulfillment of what? *The promise of the Savior.*
6. Who is Jesus' first earthly ancestor? *Adam.*
7. What was God's promise to Abraham? *He would make him into a great nation with so many descendants that they would outnumber the stars.*
8. Which two kings of the United Kingdom of Israel were Jesus' ancestors? *King David and King Solomon.*
9. Why did God split the Kingdom of Israel into northern and southern kingdoms? *Solomon built temples for his wives' false gods.*
10. Rahab was not an Israelite, but she is an ancestor of Jesus. Why? *She hid the Israelite spies from the King of Jericho and helped them escape.*

Go Further

1. What is the theme of the Old Testament? It all points to whom? (See Romans 5:12–17.)
2. What is God's plan for mankind? (See Hebrews 9:28.)
3. How do you feel when a friend stops talking to you? What could you do to get close to your friend again?
4. When you feel like God is far away, what do you do to get closer?

Wrap It Up!

Refer to the time line. From 400 B.C. to Jesus' birth, God was silent. He did not speak through his prophets. Though God was silent, he had not forgotten his people or his plan for mankind's salvation. God was working for his people, readying everything for the arrival of the promised Messiah, Jesus Christ.

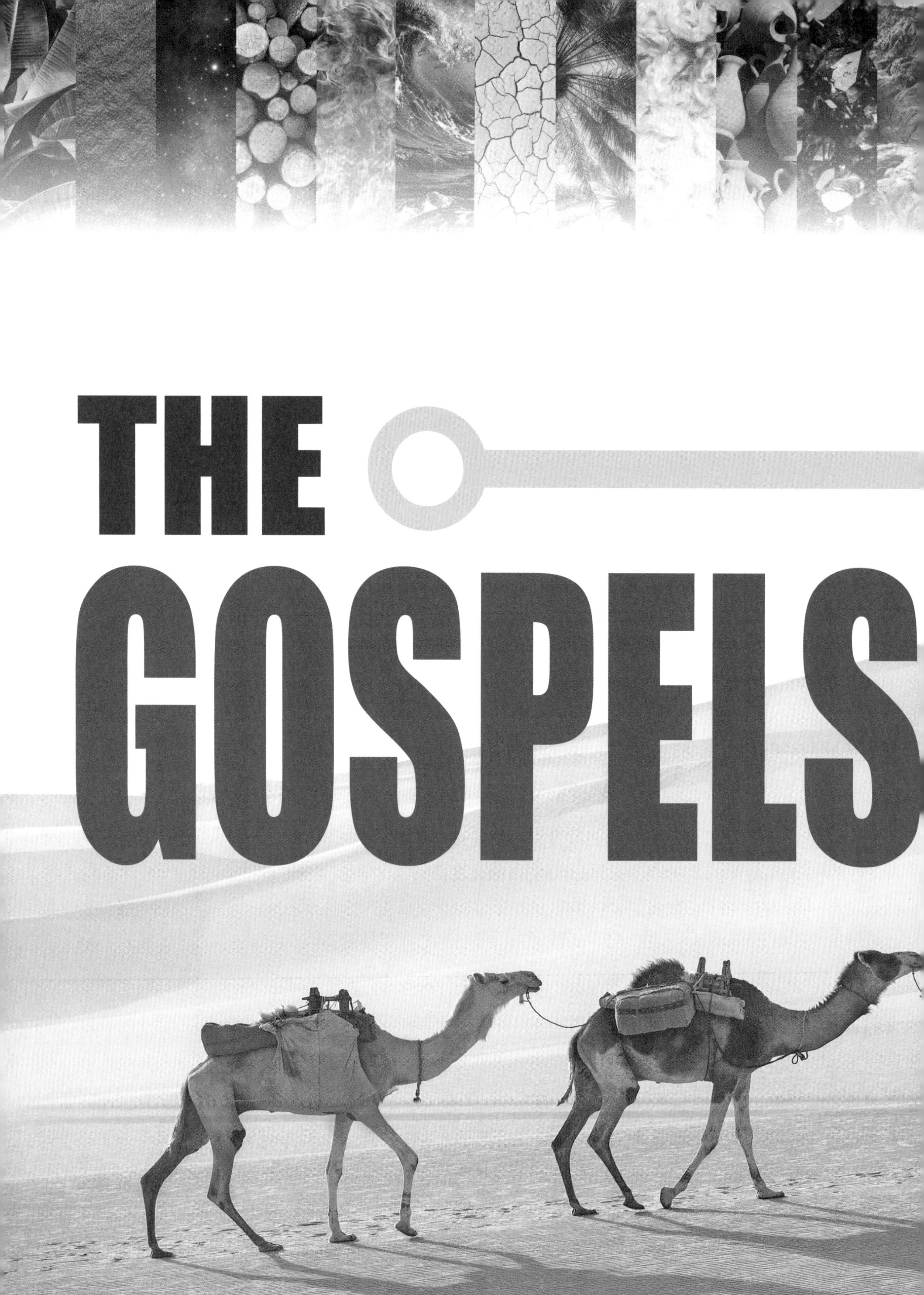
THE
GOSPELS

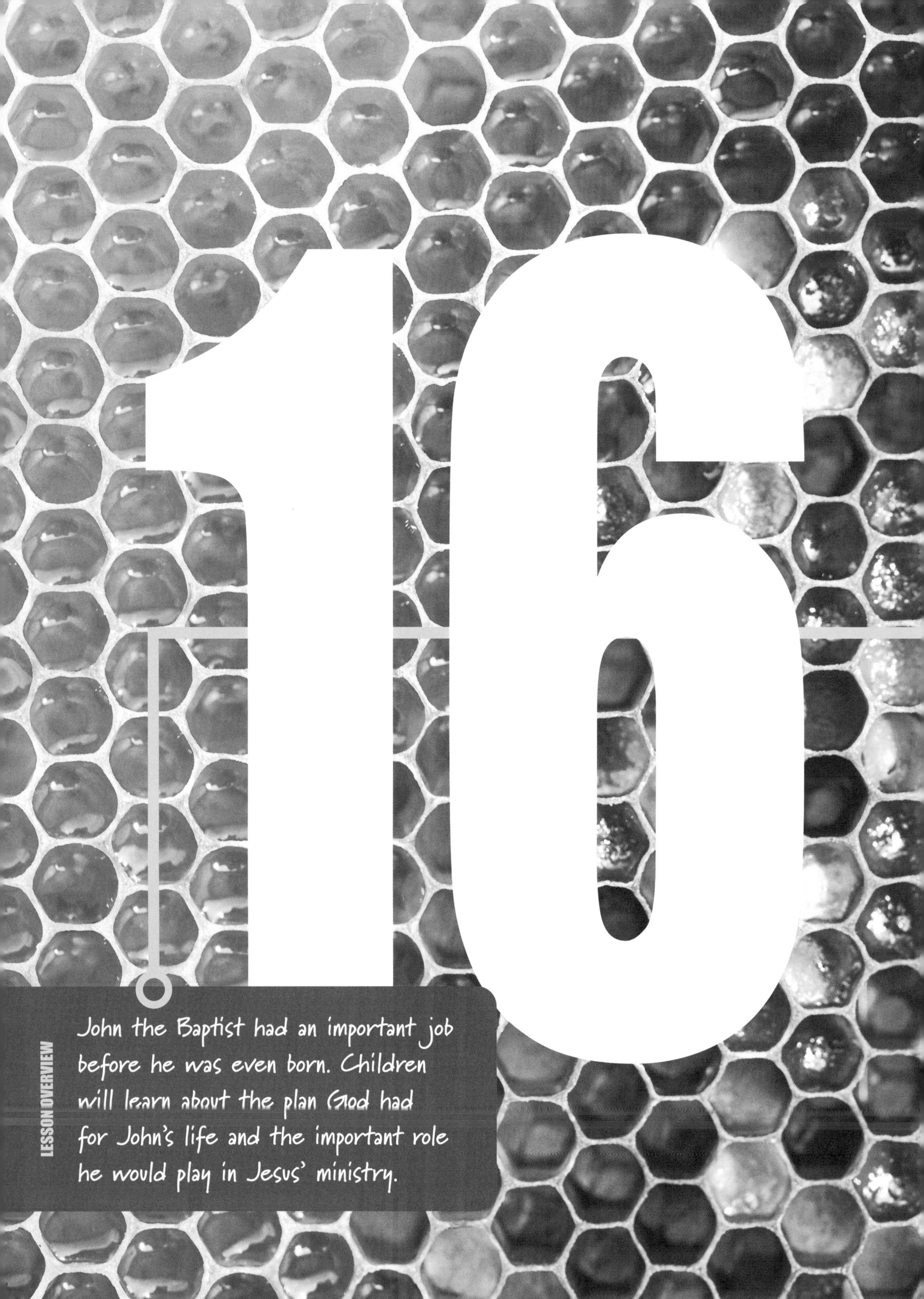

16

LESSON OVERVIEW

John the Baptist had an important job before he was even born. Children will learn about the plan God had for John's life and the important role he would play in Jesus' ministry.

Luke 1; Matthew 3:4–6,11

John the Baptist

Introduce It!

Time Line

7–5 B.C.

Key Events & People

Gabriel appears to Zechariah, birth of John; Elizabeth, Gabriel, Jesus, John, Mary, Zechariah

Memory Verse

For we are God's masterpiece. He has created us anew in Christ Jesus, so we can do the good things he planned for us long ago.

Ephesians 2:10

Time Line Materials needed. (See p. 4.)

Pray for the lesson, thanking God for each child specifically.

God is always in charge. He is never surprised by what happens. When sin entered the world, separating humanity from God, he wasn't surprised. Long before Jesus was born, God planned to send him into the world to save us from our sins. Before the time came for God to send Jesus into the world as a sacrifice for our sins, however, some things needed to happen. The Roman Empire, with its roads, common language, and stability, was important for the preparation of Jesus' coming. God also sent a special person to help prepare the way of Jesus.

Place time line marker at 7–5 B.C.

Around 7–5 B.C., God had a plan for a special baby with a special purpose. He would be Jesus' cousin, and his name was John.

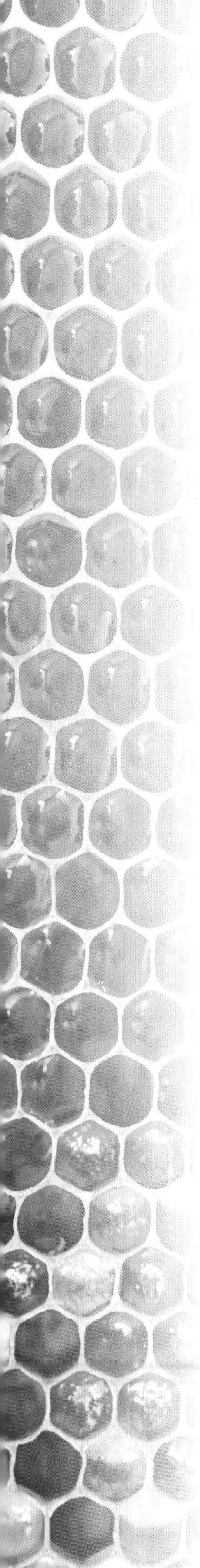

Tell It!

Choose a way to tell the story while reading the account from the Bible or telling it in your own words. Ideas for creative storytelling include acting it out, using props, or incorporating pictures.

In the Line of King David

Jesus is God's Son, but he was also fully human. He had an earthly mom and dad, just like you and me. Jesus' earthly father was a man named Joseph, and his mother was named Mary. Both Joseph and Mary came from the family line of King David. Remember the promise God made to David? Children respond. A member from David's family would sit on the throne forever. God was talking about Jesus, the King of Kings, who was from the line of David.

While explaining Jesus and John's family tree, you may wish to write out or draw pictures to illustrate.

The Birth of John the Baptist Foretold

Mary had a cousin named Elizabeth, who was married to a priest named Zechariah. They were old and had no children. One day, Zechariah was in the Temple when an angel appeared to him.

FAMILY TREE

Have each child draw their family tree as far as they can, writing down the names of each family member they know. Share family trees as time allows.

Read Luke 1:11–17.

John had an extraordinary mission for his life before he was even born! Zechariah could not believe it.

Read Luke 1:18–25.

When the angel Gabriel told Zechariah that he would have a son, he did not believe him. Zechariah could not speak the whole time Elizabeth was pregnant because of his disbelief.

Nine months later, when the baby was born. Elizabeth insisted on naming him John, but their friends and relatives

wanted to know what Zechariah wanted. The name *John* wasn't anywhere in their family tree. For the Israelites, names were very important. Being named after a family member was honorable. Raise your hand if you were named after a family member. Children respond.

It has always been common for babies to be named after family members. When Zechariah's relatives asked him what to name the baby, he still could not speak. So he wrote down on a tablet, "His name is John" (Luke 1:60). His name had been picked out by God. After Zechariah wrote this, he was able to speak again. Then, the whole family celebrated the new baby!

John the Baptist

After the miraculous naming of John, people wondered what special plans the Lord had for him. The angel Gabriel told Zechariah that John would prepare the way for Jesus and turn the hearts of the people back to the Lord. That's exactly what he did.

The book of Matthew tells us a little about the interesting way John lived.

Read Matthew 3:4–6.

His clothes and diet were a bit strange. What did he eat? Children respond. He wore clothes of camel hair and ate locust and honey. Though that's kind of crazy. What else did John do? Children respond. He baptized people! He didn't just stop there, though.

Read Matthew 3:11.

John was telling people to get ready because Jesus was literally coming!

Pray It!

Dear God, sometimes your promises seem too good to be true. Help me to believe in them always. Teach me to trust in you for my whole life. In Jesus' name, amen.

Apply It!

Choose any of these activities for your lesson. Use more than one if time allows. For any of these activities, discuss the **Talk about It!** questions on page 153 as time allows.

Show It!

Signs of Love

Overview

Children explore American Sign Language (ASL) signs and hear about John's mission to tell others about Jesus.

John the Baptist had a very important purpose: he told others to get ready for the Messiah, Jesus. Interestingly, John's father, Zechariah, lost his ability to speak for a while. How could John the Baptist have fulfilled his mission if he wasn't able to speak? Children respond. **Today, we're going to learn words in American Sign Language that we could use to tell people about Jesus. American Sign Language is a language used by people who have trouble hearing or speaking.**

Teaching Tip

Online ASL dictionaries and videos can help you learn how to do the suggested signs.

Directions

Demonstrate and lead children to repeat the following ASL signs:

1. Forgive: Stroke edge of left palm with right fingertips.
2. Jesus: One at a time, touch each palm with the opposite hand's middle finger.
3. Love: Cross fists over heart.
4. Rescue: Cross index and middle fingers of each hand; then cross and uncross hands.
5. Sin: Touch index fingertips together and then make circles with each hand.
6. Savior: Cross fists over chest, pull apart, and then move hands down sides.

Children form groups of two or three and practice using the signs they learned to tell others about Jesus.

Conversation

God had an important job for John to do. God has a plan for your life, too. One thing God wants you to do is tell others about his great love for all people and how Jesus came to save us from sin.

Act It Out!

Charades

Materials

paper scraps

pen or marker

hat, bowl, or other container

Overview

Children play a game of Charades, acting out scenes from the Bible story.

There were a number of interesting and exciting scenes from today's story. One of them involved someone not being able to speak. Let's play a game of Charades and act out scenes from the Bible story for others to guess.

Preparation

Before class, on paper scraps, write down various scenes from the Bible story. Place scraps in a hat, bowl, or other container. Use scenes such as:

- Gabriel visits Zechariah
- Zechariah can't speak
- Zechariah writing John's name on a tablet
- John eating honey and locusts
- John telling people about God
- John baptizing people

Directions

1. Children play a game of Charades, using the scenes you prepared.
2. Choose a volunteer to be "It" and pull a slip of paper from the hat, bowl, or other container.
3. "It" acts out scene without speaking until another child correctly guesses the scene. That child then becomes the new "It."
4. Continue as time and interest allow.

Conversation

It isn't always easy to get people to know what you mean when you can't use words. God knows this. That's why he gave us the Bible, which has all the words, verses, and stories we'll ever need to tell people about Jesus.

Play It!

Team Names

Materials

chairs
(1 less than the number of children)

Overview

Children play a seat-switching game based on team names as a reminder of the naming of John.

Directions

1. Place chairs in a circle, facing in.
2. Divide children into three or four teams. Ask them to choose fun team names.
3. Select one child to be "It" and stand in the middle of the circle, while the rest of the children sit in the chairs randomly, not according to their teams.

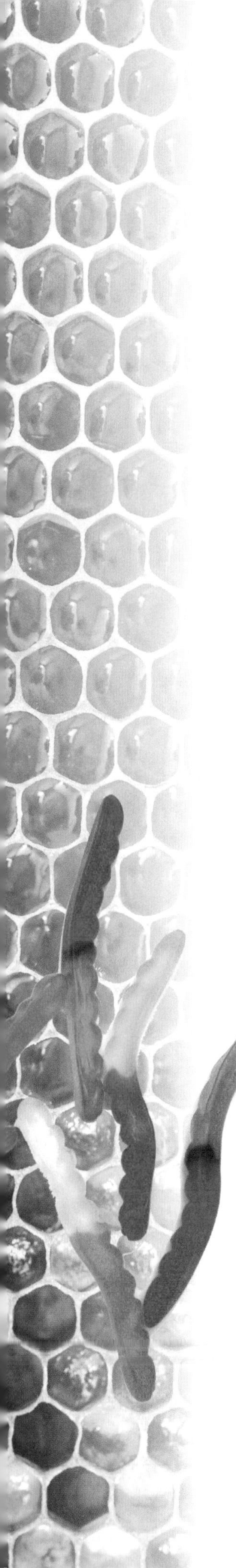

4. Call out one of the team names. Every child with that name must hop up and switch seats with someone.
5. "It" tries to grab a seat when children switch seats.
6. Player left standing in the middle becomes the new "It."

Conversation

In our game, you had to listen for your team name to know when to switch seats. Can anyone remember what was so unique about John's name? Children respond. The angel Gabriel told Zechariah what to name him. John wasn't a family name, which was uncommon at the time. God planned John's name and his life before he was born.

Craft It!

Name Art

Materials

paper

crayons or markers

Overview

Children make an acrostic with their names.

Directions

1. Children write their names in capital letters, down the left side of their papers.
2. Using the letters in their name, children write things about themselves, decorating the page. Example: Sam might write: **S**mart
   Artistic
   Musical

Conversation

John was given a special name and a special job. God had a plan for his life before he was even born. God has a plan for us, too! The Bible tells us that we are God's masterpieces. We can praise him every day for that!

Snack It!

Bugs and Honey

Materials

honey graham crackers

gummy bugs

paper plates

Overview

Children eat a snack resembling John's diet.

Directions

Children place honey graham crackers and gummy bugs on a plate and then eat their snacks.

Conversation

Who remembers what John the Baptist's very unique food choices were? Children respond. John ate locust and honey. Eewww! Thankfully, our snack today is just gummy bugs and honey cookies! Let's remember John and the work he did for Jesus while we eat our snack.

Talk about It!

1. How was Elizabeth related to Mary? *They were cousins.*
2. What was Elizabeth's husband's name? *Zechariah.*
3. Who appeared to Zechariah, telling him he would have a son? *The angel Gabriel.*
4. What was Zechariah's response to Gabriel's news? *He did not believe him.*
5. What was Zechariah's punishment for his disbelief? *He could not speak until John was born.*
6. What did John eat? *Locusts and honey.*
7. What were John's clothes made out of? *Camel hair.*
8. How did John prepare for Jesus? *He baptized people and told them he was coming.*
9. Because of the important job John had preparing the way for Jesus, he had what nickname? *John the Baptist.*

Go Further

1. Why was it so important for John to prepare the people for Jesus' coming? *So they would be ready to accept him as their Messiah.*
2. Read Mark 1:8. How did John and Jesus baptize differently? *John baptized with water, but Jesus baptized with the Holy Spirit.*

Wrap It Up!

God had a plan for Jesus to come to the world and offer true forgiveness of our sins. Things had to be just right for his arrival. God sent an angel to Zechariah to announce the good news of John's birth and life. It seemed too good to be true, and Zechariah did not believe. But God always keeps his promises. He promised that John would prepare the way for Jesus, and he did just that. John proclaimed the coming of the Messiah wherever he went and baptized those who believed.

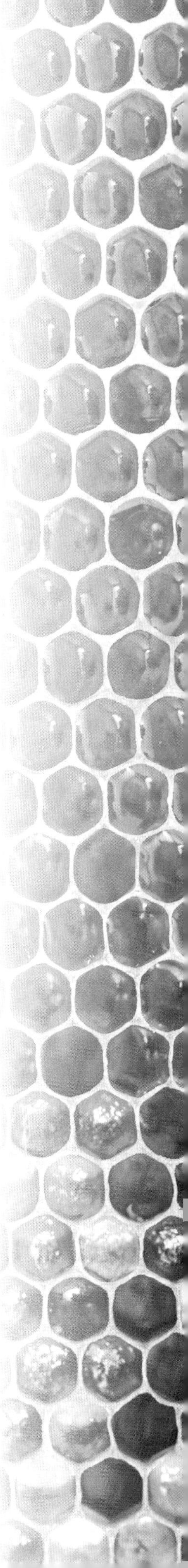

17
LESSON OVERVIEW
Jesus' birth was prophesied for thousands of years. In this chapter, children will see how God fulfilled his promises and how Jesus is our Savior.

Luke 1–2; Matthew 2

Jesus' Birth

Introduce It!

Time Line

6–4 B.C.

Key Events & People

Gabriel appears to Mary, Jesus' birth, the shepherds and wise men visit Jesus; Gabriel, Jesus, Joseph, Mary, shepherds, wise men

Memory Verse

For a child is born to us, a son is given to us . . . And he will be called: Wonderful Counselor, Mighty God, Everlasting Father, Prince of Peace.

Isaiah 9:6

Time Line Materials needed. (See p. 4.)

Pray for the lesson, thanking God for sending Jesus to Earth because of his love for us.

Jesus' birth wasn't any ordinary birth. From the beginning of time, God had a plan to save humanity from their sins. Promises and prophesies throughout the Old Testament point to the birth of Jesus. God was working and preparing for the right time. Before he could save the world, Jesus had to come to Earth.

Place time line marker at 6–4 B.C.

Around 6–4 B.C. in the little town of Bethlehem, the most famous baby was about to be born.

Tell It!

Choose a way to tell the story while reading the account from the Bible or telling it in your own words. Ideas for creative storytelling include acting it out, using props, or incorporating pictures.

The Birth of Jesus Foretold

I want you to think of the best gift you have ever received. Optional: If time allows, toss a ball or bean bag to children and have them share the best gift received.

Presents are super fun! There is one gift, though, that is the best gift ever given. Does anyone know what the gift is? Children respond. **Jesus! But why? Why is Jesus the best gift ever? To understand why Jesus is the best gift ever, we have to start back at the beginning. God created a perfect world, but then a big problem entered the world.**

Read Romans 5:12.

Sin entered the world through Adam, forever separating humans from God. But God had a plan.

Have volunteers read the following verses:

- Micah 5:2
- Isaiah 7:14
- Isaiah 9:6–7

Thousands of years before Jesus' birth, God promised that he would send a Savior. He did. And he did in the most surprising way—in the form of a tiny baby. This baby would change the world.

The Birth of Jesus

In the town of Nazareth, there was a young girl named Mary. She was engaged to a man named Joseph. One night, the angel Gabriel appeared to her. He told her not to be afraid because God loved her. God was so pleased with Mary's faith that he had chosen her to be the Messiah's mother. But Mary was confused and scared.

Read Luke 1:35–37.

Mary believed Gabriel's words and trusted in God. A few months later, Mary and Joseph traveled from Nazareth to Bethlehem for a census. Imagine going on a ninety-mile walking trip with a very pregnant woman. It was hard! Then, when they arrived in Bethlehem, there was no room for them. There was no bed or warm soup for them. An innkeeper took pity on them and gave them a stable to sleep in. That is where Jesus entered the world. In a cold, dirty, stinky stable. Mary and Joseph cherished their little baby, but they were not alone for long.

Read Luke 2: 8–18.

The shepherds were the first to see the Messiah, but they weren't the only visitors.

Kingly Guests

Some wise men from eastern lands watched the stars. One night, a new star appeared in the sky. It was a special star that they had been waiting for. They packed up their belongings and loaded their camels to follow the star. They followed the star all the way to Bethlehem to worship Jesus and give him gifts of gold, frankincense and myrrh.

Read Matthew 2:9–11.

Can you imagine receiving such expensive gifts? Mary and Joseph must have been shocked. But the greater thing to remember is that God kept all his promises. He had been telling his people for years about the Messiah. Now, those promises were being fulfilled.

Pray It!

Dear God, thank you for sending Jesus to save me from my sins. Please help me to always come to you for forgiveness when I do something wrong. In Jesus' name, amen.

Apply It!

Choose any of these activities for your lesson. Use more than one if time allows. For any of these activities, discuss the **Talk about It!** questions on page 163 as time allows.

Show It!

Materials

Advent wreath and candles

Optional: matches or lighter

Advent Wreath

Overview

Children hear about Advent wreaths and candles and learn the meaning of the word *Advent*.

Every year we all look forward to celebrating Jesus' birth at Christmas. Many people celebrate Advent as a way of looking forward to Christmas. The word *Advent* means "arrival" or "coming." Advent is celebrated on the four Sundays before Christmas.

Directions

Show children wreath and candles. **Does anyone know what this is?** Children respond. **People use Advent wreaths and candles to celebrate each Sunday of Advent. Each candle has a different meaning, which we'll learn today.** Read the meaning of each candle below. (Optional: Light each candle as you describe it's meaning. If you don't want to use open flame, you can point to each candle as you go.)

- **The first candle is lit on the first Sunday of Advent. This is the hope candle. It represents the Old Testament times when God's people hoped and prayed for the Savior God had promised to send.**
- **On the next Sunday, the peace candle is lit. It represents the peace Jesus gives to us.**
- **On the third Sunday, the joy candle is lit. It represents the joy we feel at Jesus' birth.**
- **The fourth candle, the love candle, is lit on the final Sunday before Christmas. It represents God's love for us and our love for him.**
- **Sometimes a fifth candle, a white candle called the Christ candle, is lit on Christmas Eve. It represents Jesus' birth**

Conversation

Advent not only celebrates Jesus' birth—the first time he came to Earth—but it reminds us to look forward to the day he will return!

Act It Out!

The Shepherd's Visit

Overview

Children act out the events surrounding the birth of Jesus.

> **Materials**
>
> manger (cardboard box, wicker basket, or other container)
>
> baby doll
>
> Bible-times costumes or bathrobes
>
> crowns
>
> 3 boxes wrapped in paper
>
> toy sheep (optional)

Directions

1. Choose volunteers to be Mary and Joseph. Have them dress in Bible-times costumes or bathrobes and stand at one side of the activity area with the manger and baby doll.
2. Divide the remaining children into three groups.
   - One group will act as shepherds and dress in Bible-times costumes or bathrobes.
   - Another group will be angels and wear halos and wings.
   - The third group will be the wise men wearing crowns, carrying three boxes wrapped in paper. There can be more than three wise men since the Bible does not specify how many there were.
3. The children reenact the following scenes:
   - The angels appearing to the shepherds and telling them to find the baby
   - The shepherds visiting Jesus at the manger
   - The wise men appearing with gifts
4. If you have time, choose new volunteers to be Mary and Joseph. The remaining children switch roles and repeat the activity.

Conversation

The angels visited the shepherds who were out tending their sheep in the fields, telling them about the birth of Jesus. The shepherds went right away to visit the baby Jesus. After they had visited the baby, the shepherds told everyone about what they had seen and heard! Later, the wise men appeared with gifts for Jesus.

Play It!

Pass the Present

Materials

gift-wrapped box

children's worship music and player

Overview

Children play a game like Hot Potato.

Directions

1. Children sit or stand in a circle.
2. Turn on music. As the music plays, children pass the present around the circle.
3. Stop the music. Everyone freezes. Whoever is holding the gift-wrapped box answers, or chooses a volunteer to answer, one of the discussion questions or repeats the memory verse.
4. Play continues. You may wish to periodically call out instructions such as "Switch directions," "Skip a person," etc.
5. Continue playing, repeating questions if needed, as time allows.

Conversation

Does anyone know why we receive presents at Christmastime? Children respond. **Presents at Christmastime (Jesus' birthday) remind us of the best present any of us have ever received—the gift of Jesus coming to Earth to save us from our sins!**

Craft It!

Names of Jesus

Materials

Names of Jesus (p. 161)

markers

decorating materials (stickers, glitter glue, puff paint, etc.)

Overview

Children make a word art image from the names for Jesus.

Preparation

Photocopy and enlarge to 170% the word ***Jesus*** on the right. Make one copy for each child, plus a few extras for mistakes or visitors. For each child, photocopy the Names of Jesus Chart on page 161.

Directions

1. Children write different names of Jesus inside the letters on the paper.
2. Children refer to their copy of the Names of Jesus chart as needed.

Conversation

Jesus always had a name. In fact, he has many names that we see throughout the Bible. What is your favorite name to call Jesus? Children respond.

Names of Jesus

Name	References	Meaning
Prince of Peace	Isaiah 9:6	Jesus is our peace.
Prophet	John 6:14; 7:40; Deuteronomy 18:15–22; Luke 7:16; Matthew 21:11	Jesus is the prophet foretold.
Redeemer	Job 19:25	Jesus is our redemption.
Resurrection and the Life	John 11:25	Jesus is life.
Savior	Luke 1:47—2:11; John 4:42; 1 John 4:14	Jesus is our salvation.
Shepherd	1 Peter 2:25	Jesus is the good shepherd.
Shiloh	Genesis 49:10	Jesus is our promised peace.
Son of God	Luke 1:35; Hebrews 4:14	Jesus is the Son of God by nature.
True Vine	John 15:1	Jesus is our evergreen source of life.
The Way, the Truth, and the Life	John 14:6; Acts 9:2	Jesus is our path to God.
Wisdom of God	1 Corinthians 1:24,30	Jesus is our wisdom from God.
Wonderful Counselor	Isaiah 9:6	Jesus is our defense attorney.
Word	John 1:1,14	Jesus is God's Word.
Yahweh (Jehovah)	Isaiah 40:3-5; Matthew 3:3; 28:19; Philippians 2:6-11; Exodus 3:14	Jesus has God's name.

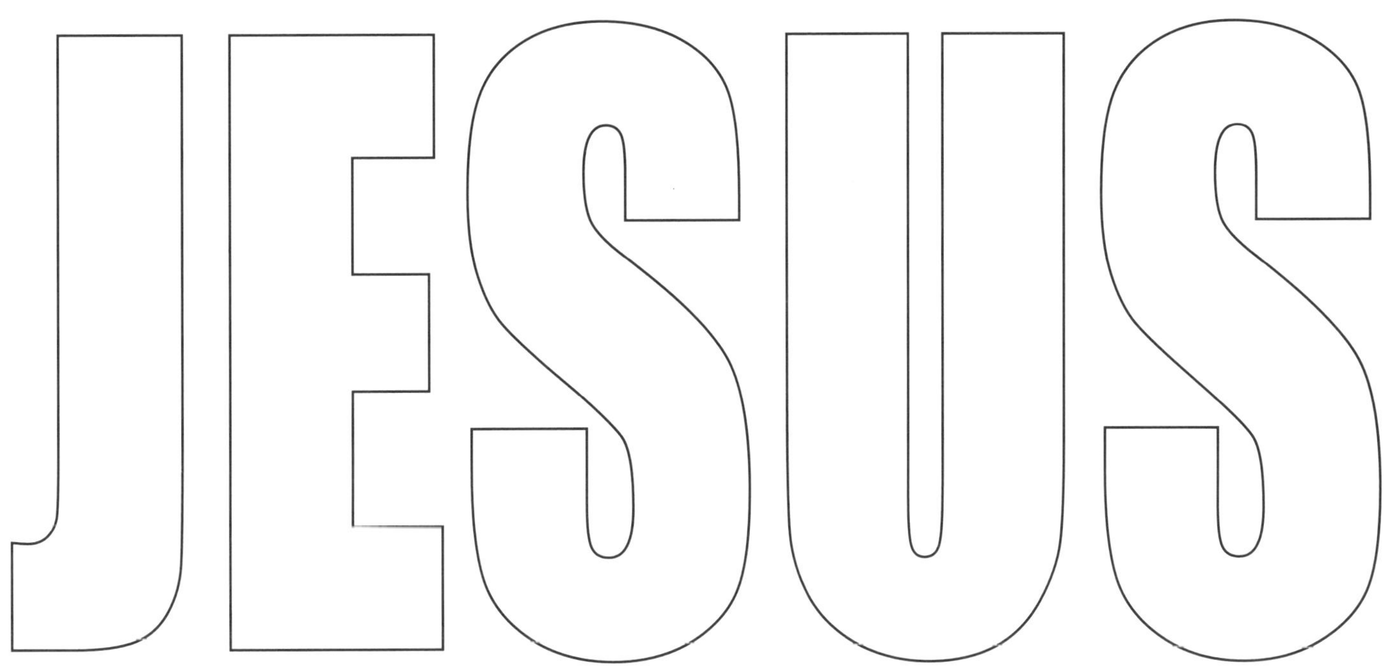

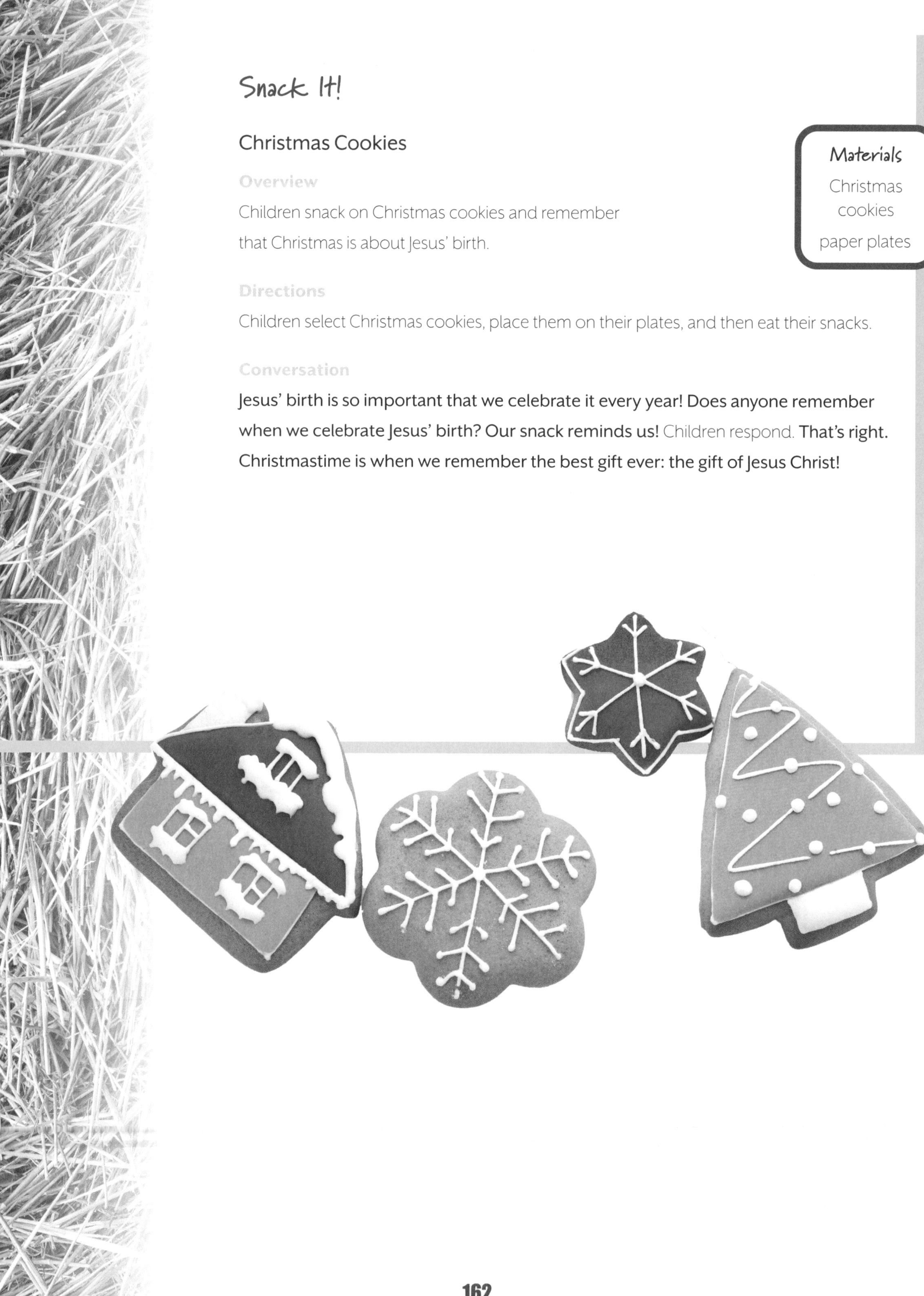

Snack It!

Christmas Cookies

Materials

Christmas cookies

paper plates

Overview

Children snack on Christmas cookies and remember that Christmas is about Jesus' birth.

Directions

Children select Christmas cookies, place them on their plates, and then eat their snacks.

Conversation

Jesus' birth is so important that we celebrate it every year! Does anyone remember when we celebrate Jesus' birth? Our snack reminds us! Children respond. **That's right. Christmastime is when we remember the best gift ever: the gift of Jesus Christ!**

Talk about It!

Basic Questions

1. What problem ruined God's perfect creation? *Sin.*
2. What was God's plan to save the world from sin? *Jesus would come to Earth to make a way for us to be forgiven for our sins.*
3. When did God make his promise to send Jesus? *Thousands of years before his birth.*
4. When was Jesus born? *6–4 B.C.*
5. What were Jesus' parents' names? *Mary and Joseph.*
6. Why were Mary and Joseph traveling? *Because of the census.*
7. Where was Jesus born? *In a stable. Bethlehem.*
8. Why was Jesus born in a stable? *There was no room for them in the inn.*
9. Who did the angels announce Jesus' birth to? *The shepherds.*
10. For what reason did Jesus come to Earth? *To save us from our sins.*

Go Further

1. What was so remarkable about Jesus being born in a stable? *God humbled himself to the lowly position of a baby, born humbly in a stable.*
2. Read Luke 19:10. Why did Jesus come to Earth? *To save the lost.*
3. What do you do to remember Christ's birth at Christmastime?

Wrap It Up!

Jesus chose to come down to Earth as a helpless baby for a reason. Because of his great love for us, he came so he could later save us from our sins. This was always God's plan to save humanity from the sin that separates us from God. Jesus' birth happened exactly as it was foretold thousands of years before. This baby, fully God but fully man, was God's gift to us, offering the way for forgiveness for our sins!

18
LESSON OVERVIEW
Through the baptism of Jesus, children will learn about baptism and the significance of Jesus' baptism.

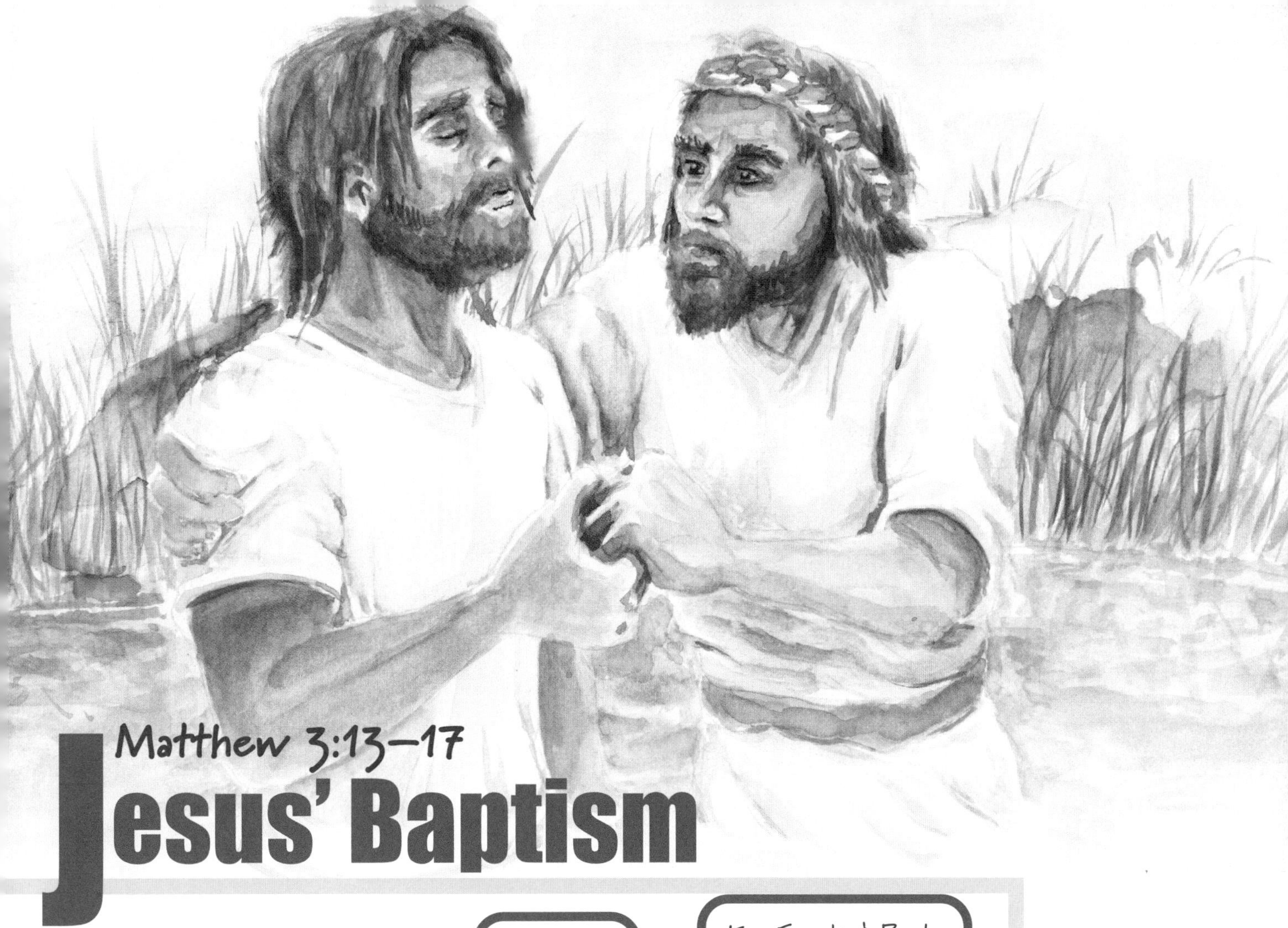

Matthew 3:13–17

Jesus' Baptism

Introduce It!

Time Line

26 A.D.

Key Events & People

Jesus' Baptism; Jesus, John the Baptist

Memory Verse

Anyone who believes and is baptized will be saved. But anyone who refuses to believe will be condemned.

Mark 16:16

Time Line Materials needed. (See p. 4.)

Pray for the lesson, asking the Holy Spirit to speak to any kids who have not yet accepted Christ as their Lord and Savior.

Jesus is born! The Savior has come to Earth! The Bible doesn't tell us much about Jesus's childhood. Luke 2:41–52 tells us that when Jesus was twelve, he went to the Temple and taught people about God. "All who heard him were amazed at his understanding and his answers" (Luke 2:47). But the rest of his childhood remains a mystery.

Place time line marker at 26 A.D.

When Jesus was around thirty to thirty-two years old, around 26 A.D., he began his ministry. He started off with an encounter with his cousin, John the Baptist.

Tell It!

Choose a way to tell the story while reading the account from the Bible or telling it in your own words. Ideas for creative storytelling include acting it out, using props, or incorporating pictures.

A Sin Problem

Genesis 1 tells us about the world that God created. Does anyone remember what God said after everything he created? Children respond. It was "very good." The world that God created was perfect.

Does anyone know why sin is a problem? Children respond. Sin separates us from God. Everyone sins (Romans 3:23). Because we sin, we deserve punishment (Romans 6:23). We deserve death and eternal separation from our Holy God because of our sin. How do we get rid of our sin so that we can be with God?

John Baptizes Jesus

The whole reason Jesus came to Earth was to fix our sin problem. Before it was time for him to die on the cross, saving us from our sins, he had to get things ready. Jesus began his ministry on Earth with a meeting with his cousin, John.

Who remembers what John's life mission was? Children respond. He prepared the way for the Lord. One day, John was preaching about the coming Messiah when Jesus arrived. Jesus asked John to baptize him the same way he had been baptizing other believers. John was shocked.

"John tried to talk him out of it. 'I am the one who needs to be baptized by you,' he said, 'so why are you coming to me?'" (Matthew 3:14). Jesus told him that it was what God required him to do. John obeyed and baptized him.

When Jesus came up and out of the water, an amazing thing happened. "The heavens were opened and he saw the Spirit of God descending like a dove and settling on him. And a voice from heaven said, 'This is my dearly loved Son, who brings me great joy'" (Matthew 3:16–17).

Can you imagine hearing a voice from heaven? Everyone must have been amazed. Their Messiah was here! The Heavens had just declared it.

Baptism of the Holy Spirit

What happened after Jesus was baptized? What descended on him? Children respond. **The Holy Spirit. Who is the Holy Spirit?** Children respond. **The Holy Spirit is the third part of the trinity. John told people that while he baptized with water, Jesus would baptize with the Spirit (see Matthew 3:11).**

After a person repents and follows Jesus, they receive the Holy Spirit. The Holy Spirit is the part of the Trinity remaining with us now on Earth until Jesus comes back. Each and every one of us who believes in Jesus and confesses their sins will be saved, receiving the Holy Spirit to guide us and lead us.

Pray It!

Dear God, thank you for giving us the Holy Spirit so that we know we are never alone. Thank you for thinking that we are so important that you would send Jesus to save us. In Jesus' name, amen.

Apply It!

Choose any of these activities for your lesson. Use more than one if time allows. For any of these activities, discuss the **Talk about It!** questions on page 171 as time allows.

Show It!

Materials
dirty drinking glass
bowl of soapy water
sponge
towel

Dirty v. Clean

Overview

Clean a dirty glass to demonstrate how baptism is a symbolic way of showing we've been forgiven for our sins.

Let's look at something that reminds us of one way we can show we follow Jesus.

Directions

1. Show the dirty drinking glass. **Raise your hand if you'd like me to get a drink of water for you from this glass.** Children respond. **What? No one wants to drink from this glass? What if it was chocolate milk instead of water? Still no one?** Children respond.
2. Wash glass in soapy water and dry with towel. **How about now? Would any of you drink from this glass?** Children respond. **We use water to clean glasses and dishes. We also use water to clean our clothes, our pets, and even our bodies! The Bible often compares washing with water to baptism. Baptism represents how when we become members of God's family, God forgives our sins. We are essentially cleaned from sin.**

Enrichment Idea

Invite a pastor to come to your class and explain the baptism method used at your church.

Conversation

When Jesus was baptized, God was pleased and told everyone that Jesus is his Son. Baptism is a way for us to tell others that we are members of God's family, too. We are showing that we have been cleansed from sin and that we love and follow Jesus.

Act It Out!

Materials
Bibles
Bible-times costumes (optional)

John Baptizes Jesus

Overview

Children use words from the Bible to act out the baptism of Jesus.

Directions

1. Children form pairs. Give each pair a Bible opened to Matthew 3:13–17.
2. One person in each group will pretend to be Jesus and read the words from the Bible that were spoken by Jesus. The other person in each pair will be John the Baptist and read his words. If you have an odd number of children, choose one to be the voice of God in verse 17; otherwise, read the lines for God yourself.
3. Children pretending to be Jesus will start things off by asking John to baptize them. Since these words are not in the Bible passage, have each child say, "John, I want you to baptize me."
4. After reading the verses, partners swap roles. You may also wish to change up the pairs.

Conversation

Imagine what John must have thought when he was the one asked to baptize Jesus, the Son of God! What must he have felt? Jesus would later die on the cross to save us from our sins. Jesus was the only person who could do that because he had never sinned. If Jesus never sinned, why do you think he wanted to be baptized?

Play It!

Triangle Trio

Materials
pool noodle (1 per child)

Overview

Children play a game to remind them of the Trinity.

Directions

1. Divide children into groups of three. If you don't have a number of kids that divides evenly into three, you may have to form one group of four.
2. Give each player a pool noodle.
3. Groups of three form triangles and stand their noodle in front of them. Noodles must stand straight up and down. The noodles will not change positions.
4. On your signal, each player lets go of their noodle, rotates one place to the left in their triangle, and grabs the noodle there without letting it fall down.
5. Any team that drops one or more noodles answers one of the **Talk about It!** questions on page 171.

Conversation

What a fun game! Can anyone think of why we played the game standing in a triangle? Children respond. **Triangles remind us of the Trinity—God in three parts, the Father, the Son, and the Holy Spirit. All three of the parts of God were there when Jesus was baptized!**

Craft It!

Trinity Triangles

Materials

markers

decorating materials (stickers, craft-foam shapes, glitter glue, etc.)

Overview

Children draw triangles and decorate them to remind them of the Trinity.

Directions

1. Give each child a sheet of paper. Children draw a large triangle.
2. Children label the three sides of the triangle:
   - The Father is God.
   - Jesus is God.
   - The Holy Spirit is God.
3. Children use decorative materials to decorate their triangles.

Conversation

You wrote on your triangles the names of the three parts of the trinity. Each part is fully God! Which ones were there when Jesus was baptized? Children respond. **All of them! We can feel good knowing that all believers receive the Spirit, just like Jesus!**

Snack It!

Berry Blue Gelatin

Materials

individual blue gelatin snacks

variety of berries

plastic spoons

Overview

Children will enjoy a snack that looks like and is made from water, reminding them of Jesus' baptism.

Jesus was baptized in the Jordan River. Today's snack reminds us of the river where Jesus was baptized. It looks like water and is made with water!

Directions

1. Give each child a gelatin snack.
2. Place berries where children can reach them. They can choose berries to top their gelatin snacks.

Conversation

Put your hand on your head if you've been baptized. Tell the group what getting baptized was like, [Ethan].

Talk about It!

Basic Questions

1. How are Jesus and John the Baptist related? *They are cousins.*
2. The perfect world described in Genesis 1 is free from what? *Sin.*
3. What is the problem with sin? *It separates us from God.*
4. How can our sins be forgiven? *Through Jesus' death and resurrection on the cross.*
5. How old was Jesus when he started his ministry?
   Around thirty to thirty-two years old.
6. Jesus asked John the Baptist to do what? *To baptize him.*
7. What was John's response to Jesus' request?
   John thought that he should be the one baptized by Jesus.
8. What descended on Jesus after he was baptized? *The Holy Spirit.*
9. Who is the Holy Spirit? *God; part of the Trinity.*
10. When does a person receive the Holy Spirit? *When they repent and are baptized.*

Go Further

1. Why was Jesus baptized? *To fulfill righteousness; to set the example for us.*
2. What does baptism represent? *It's a public declaration of a personal transformation.*
3. How many members of the Trinity were present during Jesus baptism? *All three.*

Wrap It Up!

Jesus began his earthly ministry by being baptized. He was baptized to fulfill all righteousness and to set the example for us, though Jesus did not sin or need repentance. Just as the Holy Spirit descended upon Jesus after his baptism, all believers also receive the Holy Spirit to lead us and guide us.

19

LESSON OVERVIEW

Children will discover why Jesus was put to death, why there was a guard placed at his tomb, and why he had to die.

Matthew 26:36–56; 27:32–65; Luke 23:26—24:12

Jesus' Death and Resurrection

Introduce It!

Time Line

30 A.D.

Key Events & People

Jesus' death, burial, and resurrection; Jesus, Joseph of Arimathea, Pharisees, Pilate

Memory Verse

He himself is the sacrifice that atones or our sins—and not only our sins but the sins of all the world.

1 John 2:2

Time Line Materials needed. (See p. 4.)

Start the lesson in prayer, confessing any sins and thanking Jesus for dying on the cross for us, forgiving our sins.

After the birth of Jesus, around 6–4 B.C. (refer to time line), there is one story about Jesus as a boy in the Temple. We know nothing else until he began his ministry around 26 A.D. (refer to time line). During his ministry, Jesus traveled around healing people, performing miracles, and teaching the Word of God. Many people became followers of God during this time, but there was one group of people who did not like Jesus.

The Pharisees studied the Old Testament scriptures. They knew all about the prophets and about the coming Messiah. But they did not believe Jesus was the Messiah they were waiting for. They felt threatened by the message he spoke.

Place time line marker at 30 A.D. Around 30 A.D., the Pharisees thought they found a way to stop the message of Christ from spreading.

Tell It!

Choose a way to tell the story while reading the account from the Bible or telling it in your own words. Ideas for creative storytelling include acting it out, using props, or incorporating pictures.

Garden of Gethsemane

One of the attributes of God is that he is *omniscient*, meaning he knows everything.

- Jesus knew why he was sent to Earth.
- He knew what was going to happen.
- He knew who his twelve followers (disciples) would be.
- He knew they would travel with him all over Judea.
- He knew that one of them would betray him.

What does *betray* mean? Children respond. It means purposely destroying someone's trust. Jesus even warned Judas (his disciple) that he would be the one to betray him.

As the time for Jesus' death approached, he went to a garden to pray and spend time with God the Father.

Read Matthew 26:39.

What did Jesus pray in the garden? Children respond. He asked God if there was any way for this cup to pass him. He wanted to know if there was another way to save the world from sin. He was scared to die. He wanted to be absolutely, positively sure that this was the ONLY way. Even so, Jesus also told God that what he wanted was as important as what God needed him to do. Even though he didn't want to die, Jesus went ahead with God's plan willingly.

While he prayed, Judas arrived with a group of soldiers to arrest Jesus. Judas had betrayed Jesus, just as Jesus had predicted.

The soldiers did not have to use violence or force when arresting Jesus. They did not drag him kicking and screaming. He simply went with them. Why? He is all powerful, so he did not have to go with the crowd. He hadn't done anything wrong, nothing to deserve being arrested.

Guards at the Tomb

Jesus was arrested and stood trial under Pontius Pilate, the Roman governor. He was sentenced to be hanged on a cross alongside two other criminals. The Roman soldiers hurt Jesus badly and put a crown of thorns on his head. Jesus died on that cross for all the sins of the whole world. When he died, the sky darkened, rocks split apart, the earth rumbled, and the curtain in the Temple ripped. The Roman soldiers said to each other, "This man truly was the Son of God" (Matthew 27:54).

After Jesus died, he was placed in the tomb of a man named Joseph of Arimathea. Back then, they placed people who had died in caves. Jesus' tomb had a soldier stationed outside to guard it. Isn't it strange to guard a dead person? Why do you think there were guards outside? Children respond.

Read Matthew 27:62–66.

Jesus had been telling people that after three days, he would rise from the dead. The Pharisees did not believe him, but they were afraid that Jesus' disciples would steal his body. The Pharisees thought they would try to trick everyone into thinking that he was the Son of God.

Jesus' Resurrection

Read Luke 24:1–12.

When the women got to the tomb, what did they find? Children respond. It was empty! Jesus was gone! He died to take the punishment for our sins, but he did not stay dead, just as he said!

Pray It!

Dear God, thank you for dying for my sins. Thank you for loving me even though I do wrong things. Teach me to love others who wrong me also. In Jesus' name, amen.

Apply It!

Choose any of these activities for your lesson. Use more than one if time allows. For any of these activities, discuss the **Talk about It!** questions on page 181 as time allows.

Show It!

> **Materials**
>
> Two each of several examples of fruits with pits, or seeds (peaches, apricots, plums, avocados, olives, etc.)
>
> knife (for adult use only)

Seed to Believe

Overview

Children examine fruit pits and discuss whether pits are dead or alive.

Preparation

For each type of fruit that you gathered, cut one open to remove the seed. Keep the seed and the other, whole fruit. Discard (or set aside to eat) the cut fruit.

In today's Bible story, everyone KNEW Jesus was dead. So imagine how surprised they felt when they saw he was alive! I'm going to show you some things, and I want you to decide if they are dead or alive.

Directions

1. Show children each of the fruit seeds. **What do you think this is? A seed? What kind of seed?** Children respond. **This seed looks small, dried-up . . . It doesn't have anything green or flowerful or fruit-like about it. Do you think this seed is dead or alive? Why?** Children respond.
2. **Each of these seeds is from one of these fruits.** Show children the different fruit for each pit. **Which of these seeds belongs to which of these fruits?** Children respond.
3. After children have finished guessing, slice open the whole fruits to show if they correctly identified each seed.

Conversation

These seeds may not look alive, but there is life inside of them. What are some of the things a seed needs to grow into a plant that bears fruit like these? Children respond. **If planted, watered, and given the right amount of sunshine and care, these seeds can grow into big plants and trees that can grow even more fruit with more seeds!**

When Jesus died on the cross, his friends thought that he was dead forever. But Jesus is alive! He rose from the tomb, and he's alive today. And when we believe in him, we can have eternal life. That's a whole lot of life-giving from one death!

Act It Out!

Materials

Bible

Optional: Bible-times costumes

Jesus' Resurrection

Today we are going to reenact the resurrection of Jesus!

Overview

Children act out the account of Jesus' resurrection.

Directions

1. Assign each child to a role or two to play in the reenactment of the resurrection scene. You can assign more than one role if your class is small, or double the roles if your class is big. You will need:
   - Joseph
   - Pilate
   - 3 women
   - 2 angels
   - Peter and other disciples
2. Read, or choose a volunteer to read, Luke 23:50—24:12 as children act out the story action.

Conversation

Jesus died on a cross to save us from our sins. The good news, however, is that he didn't stay dead! He rose from the tomb and because he did, we can be forgiven of our sins and become members of God's family. That is the good news of the gospel!

Play It!

Stand Up If It's True

Overview

Children stand or sit to indicate whether statements about the Bible story are true or false.

Directions

Read the statements below. Children stand up if they think the statement is true but sit down if they think it is false. If an answer is false, ask a volunteer to explain why it is false.

1. Healing people was against the law.
   False. There is no law against helping or healing people.
2. Teaching from God's Word was against the law.
   False. There is no law against teaching from God's Word.
3. Jesus preached God's Word. *True.*
4. Jesus picked fights with the religious leaders.
   False. Jesus showed patience and peace.
5. Jesus' followers were not breaking laws. *True.*
   Though Peter did cut the soldier's ear off.
6. The religious leaders had been trying to arrest Jesus from the beginning of his ministry. *True.*
7. Jesus did not follow the laws. *False. Jesus never sinned—and that includes never breaking laws.*
8. It was against the law for someone to claim they are God.
   False. But it did make people mad!
9. Jesus treated everyone kindly. *True.*
10. Jesus was arrested and killed even though he had done nothing wrong. *True.*

Conversation

Jesus broke no laws during his ministry, but he was arrested and killed anyway. Jesus knew it was to happen this way, and he willingly sacrificed himself. He knew it was the only way to save us from the penalty for our sins. That's amazing love!

Craft It!

Toothpick Crosses

Overview

Children make crosses as reminders of Jesus' death and resurrection.

Today, we heard about Jesus' death on a wooden cross. We're going to make crosses made from wood—wooden toothpicks!

Materials

black construction paper

pencils

craft or white glue

round toothpicks

Directions

1. On a sheet of black construction paper, each child draws the shape of a cross.
2. Children fill their crosses with glue.
3. Children lay toothpicks in the glue to fill in their crosses.
4. Once dry, children can cut out their crosses, or keep them on the black background.

Optional Ideas:

- Use colored toothpicks instead of plain ones.
- After glue dries, children paint crosses with gold or silver paint.
- Attach magnets or yarn loops to crosses to make them easy to display.
- Children decorate crosses with small fabric flowers as a reminder of the gardens where Jesus prayed and where he was buried, purple fabric as a reminder of the Temple's torn curtain, or circles of raffia to represent the crown of thorns.

Conversation

Remembering Jesus' death is a way to honor the love he showed us by being willing to die for us. Remembering Jesus' resurrection is a way to remember God's amazing power. Because Jesus died and rose again, we can be forgiven for our sin and become members of God's family. What an awesome gift! What can you do or say to show that you are grateful for Jesus' death and resurrection?

Snack It!

Cross Crackers

Overview

Children make snacks with crosses to remind them of Jesus' death on the cross.

Materials

graham crackers
paper plates (1 per child)
frosting
craft sticks (1 per child)
M&M candies

Directions

1. Give each child a graham cracker square on a paper plate.
2. Hand each child a craft stick with some frosting on it.
3. Children spread the frosting on the graham cracker and then arrange M&Ms on the frosting in a cross shape.

Conversation

Our snack today has the shape of a cross. The cross is a reminder of what Jesus did for us and the sacrifice he willingly made so that we can become members of God's family.

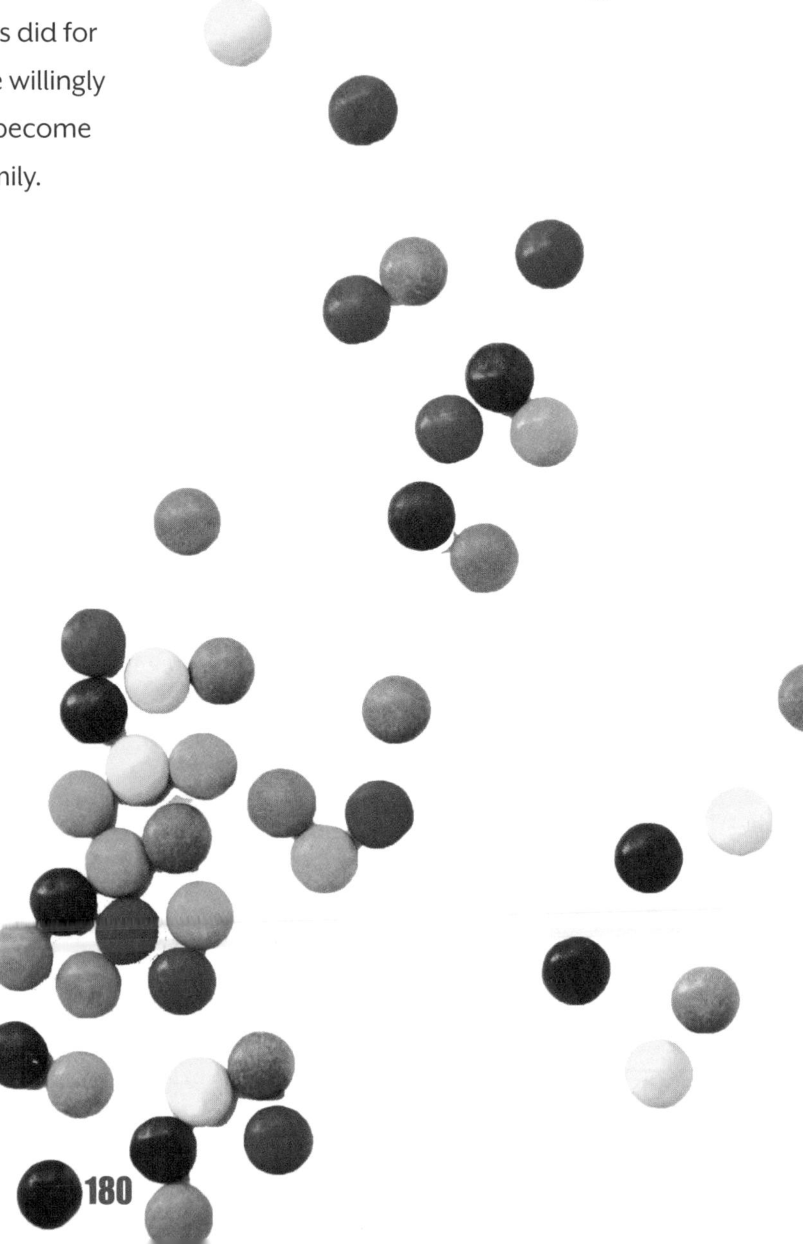

Talk about It!

Basic Questions

1. What group of people wanted Jesus killed? *The Pharisees.*
2. Jesus stood trial under who? *Pilate, the Roman governor.*
3. How many days was Jesus dead? *Three.*
4. Whose tomb was Jesus buried in? *Joseph of Arimathea.*
5. What was placed outside Jesus' tomb? *A guard.*
6. Why was there a guard outside Jesus' tomb? *The Pharisees were afraid the disciples would steal his body and say he'd resurrected.*
7. What did the women find when they arrived at the tomb on the third day? *The tomb was empty.*
8. Who appeared to the women outside of the tomb? *Two angels.*
9. What was the disciples' reaction to the news that Jesus was alive? *They did not believe the women at first.*
10. Why did Jesus have to die? *To offer forgiveness for our sins.*

Go Further

1. What happened when Jesus died? (See Matthew 27:50–54.) *The curtain in the Temple ripped, the earth shook, rocks split apart, tombs opened, etc.*
2. What was so important about the fact that Jesus did not stay dead? *He fulfilled the prophecies.*
3. How did Jesus' death and resurrection affect you? What does it mean to you?

Wrap It Up!

Refer to the time line.

Though Jesus never did anything wrong or broke any laws, he was arrested, tried, and found guilty. He was sentenced to death, beaten, crucified, and laid in a tomb. He did not, however, stay dead. Jesus' death and resurrection took place to fulfill the scriptures and to offer forgiveness of our sins. Jesus' death and resurrection was the ultimate sacrifice, the atoning sacrifice, paying the price for our sins and granting eternal life to all who believe.

LETTERS, AND

HISTORY, PROPHESY

20

LESSON OVERVIEW

Children will learn what happened to turn Paul from a persecutor of Christians to an influential God follower!

Acts 9
Paul's Conversion

Introduce It!

Time Line
38 A.D.

Key Events & People
Paul blinded on the road to Damascus; Ananias, Paul

Memory Verse
Live a life filled with love, following the example of Christ.
Ephesians 5:2

Time Line Materials needed. (See p. 4.)

Begin the lesson in prayer, asking God to help us to follow him with our hearts and actions.

After Jesus' death and resurrection around 30 A.D. (refer to time line), the spread of the gospel and the birth of the church began. Jesus' followers traveled around and told EVERYONE about him. But not everyone was happy about it.

Do you remember the whole reason Jesus was put to death? Children respond. The Pharisees thought they could stop his message by killing him. Even after Jesus resurrected and went back to Heaven, there were groups of people trying to stop the spread of the gospel.

Place time line marker at 38 A.D.

That is where we are now, in 38 A.D., a few years after Jesus' death and resurrection, where we will meet an influential man.

Tell It!

Choose a way to tell the story while reading the account from the Bible or telling it in your own words. Ideas for creative storytelling include acting it out, using props, or incorporating pictures.

Who Is Paul?

Start the lesson with the game What is Different on page 188.

WHAT IS DIFFERENT

Paul (also called Saul) was possibly one of the most influential people, other than Jesus, in the Bible. What kind of a guy do you think he was? Children respond. Let's see if what you think matches what the Bible says about Paul.

Read Acts 8:3.

Paul was not a good guy. He was a very faithful student of the Bible teachings, but he did not believe that Jesus was the Messiah. Because of that, he made it his mission to kill and imprison Christians wherever he went.

Paul was so sure that these Christians were wrong that he wrote letters to the synagogues. Synagogues are places where Jews worship God. Paul asked for their help. He wanted to rally more people to capture and arrest these Christians. He wanted to bring them back to Jerusalem in chains and make an example out of them.

On the Road to Damascus

One day, Paul was on the road to Damascus to capture Christians. Suddenly, a light from Heaven burst through the clouds. It was so strong that it blinded him! Paul fell off his steed and onto the ground.

Read Acts 9:4–6.

Jesus spoke directly to Paul! He wanted Paul to stop hurting his believers. Paul could hardly believe what happened. He was speechless and he couldn't see anything. The people he was traveling with led him the rest of the way to Damascus. For three days, he was blind.

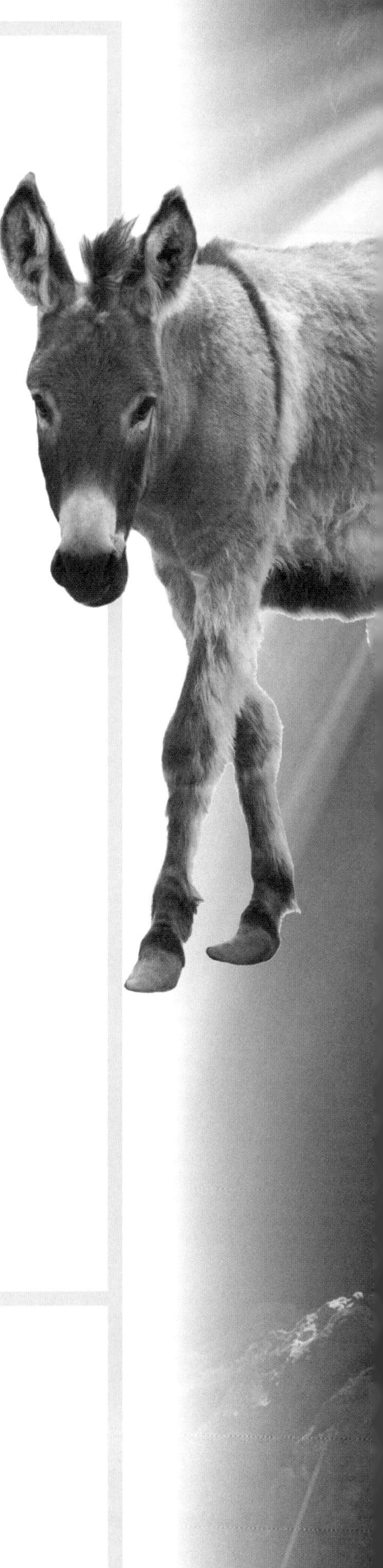

Paul Is Changed

God sent Ananias, a follower of Christ, to heal Paul's eyesight. At first Ananias was confused. He said to God, "I've heard many people talk about the terrible things this man has done to the believers in Jerusalem! And he is authorized by the leading priests to arrest everyone who calls upon your name" (Acts 9:13–14). Ananias was scared of getting arrested. Why should he heal a man who was persecuting his fellow believers?

God assured Ananias that Paul was a changed man and that he was going to use him to do great things for the Kingdom of God. Ananias obeyed God and went to Paul.

Read Acts 9:17–18.

As soon as Paul regained his strength, he went to the synagogues and preached about Jesus! He told everyone he saw about his experience with the true God! The people were amazed. They asked each other, "Isn't this the same man who caused such devastation among Jesus' followers in Jerusalem? . . . And didn't he come here to arrest them and take them in chains to the leading priests?" (Acts 9:21).

The people were shocked by Paul's change of heart. He became a powerful speaker about Jesus. This angered some of the Jews, so they made a plan to kill him. But Paul was warned of this plan, and he escaped safely to Jerusalem.

God had big plans for Paul. A former persecutor of Christians had been changed in a big way!

Pray It!

Dear God, thank you for changing our hearts every day. Sometimes we think we know what is right, but really we need to listen to you. Teach us how to listen to you always. In Jesus' name, amen.

Apply It!

Choose any of these activities for your lesson. Use more than one if time allows. For any of these activities, discuss the **Talk about It!** questions on page 191 as time allows.

Show It!

What Is Different?

Materials

stopwatch or watch with second hand

Overview

Children try to guess what is different about their friend's appearance.

Directions

1. Select a volunteer to stand in front of the group.
2. Give the remaining children twenty to thirty seconds to memorize every detail of the child's appearance.
3. Out of eyesight of the other children, behind a screen or in the hallway with an adult helper, subtly change one detail of the volunteer's appearance. For example, change hair from a ponytail to pigtails, button a shirt wrong, switch a bracelet to another hand, put shoes on the wrong feet, take off socks or a scarf, etc.
4. Volunteer returns to stand in front of the class and have the other children try to guess what is different. When a child correctly guesses the difference, guesser answers, or chooses a volunteer to answer, one of the **Talk about It!** questions on page 191.
5. Continue play with different volunteers as time and interest allow.

Conversation

Did you find it easy to find the differences in our friends' appearances? Why or why not? Children respond. **If I came in here with purple hair, you would probably notice, but you might not notice if I just got a trim. Big differences are pretty easy to see.**

After Paul met Jesus on the road to Damascus, what kind of change do you think he had? A big change or a small change? Why?

Act It Out!

On the Road

Materials

Large, bright flashlight (like a scuba light) or work light

Optional: Bible-times costumes

Overview

Children reenact Paul's conversion on the way to Damascus.

Directions

Lead children to do motions along with you as you briefly retell the story (See Acts 9).

- For walking to Damascus, have children walk in place.
- For when the bright light appears, turn on the flashlight and have children fall to the ground.
- For Paul being blinded, have children stand and walk (carefully!) with their eyes closed.
- Act as Ananias and place a hand on each child's head. When you do, they can open their eyes and see again.

Conversation

Paul was traveling to Damascus on his way to persecute Christians when God stopped him and changed him. God had a big plan for Paul's life. God has a big plan for your life, too!

Play It!

Walk the Road

construction paper or masking tape to create a path

blindfolds

Overview

Children complete a relay race while being blindfolded.

Preparation

Before class, lay sheets of construction paper or use masking tape to make two identical paths across the play area.

Directions

1. Have children pair up and then divide into two teams. Teams line up by pairs at the beginning of one of the paths.
2. On your signal, one member of the first pair in each team blindfolds their partner and then leads partner to follow the path you made using only their voice.
3. When a blindfolded player gets to the end of the path, they take off the blindfold and then put it on their partner. The blindfolded partner is then given directions to follow the path back to the beginning.
4. When the team returns to the beginning, the blindfold is handed off to the next pair who repeat the action.
5. The first team to finish the relay answers one of the **Talk about It!** questions on page 191.
6. Repeat relay, making new partners and teams as time and interest allow.

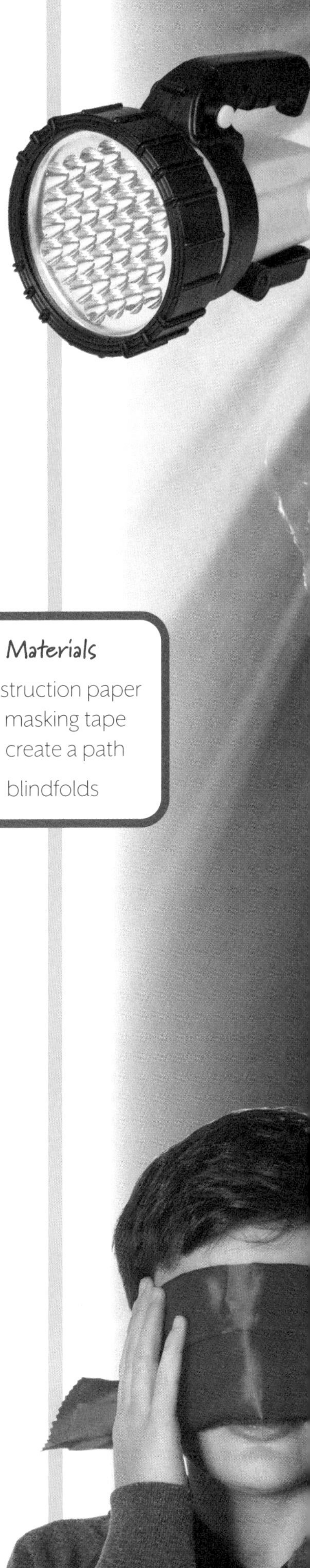

Conversation

Was it hard or easy to walk along the road blindfolded? Children respond. **Imagine being suddenly blind for three whole days like Paul was! What else would be difficult to do?**

Craft It!

Paper Faces

Materials

paper plate
crayons or markers
drinking straw
masking tape

Overview

Children make a craft with happy and angry faces to show Paul's conversion.

Directions

1. Give each child a paper plate.
2. On one side of the paper plate, children draw a happy face. On the other side, children draw an angry face.
3. Children then tape a drinking straw to the bottom of the paper plate.
4. Children spin the straw in their hands to watch the faces change.

Conversation

How was Paul changed after what happened to him on the way to Damascus? Children respond. **Paul went from being an angry man to being a happy man! He was so different that people could not believe he was the same man!**

Snack It!

Salty Sweet Popcorn

Materials

caramel and white cheddar popcorn
small paper cups

Overview

Children taste and discuss the difference between two different flavors of popcorn.

Directions

1. Give each child a small paper cup, filled with each flavor of popcorn.
2. Encourage children to try each type of popcorn separately, and then together.

Conversation

Can you taste the difference between the two types of popcorn in our snack today? Children respond. **The white cheddar popcorn is salty, while the caramel popcorn is sweet! The difference in the taste of our popcorn reminds us of the difference in Paul before Damascus and after! He was a completely different man after he met God on the road!**

Talk about It!

Basic Questions

1. At first, what did Paul plan to do to the Christians? *Arrest and imprison them.*
2. Whose permission did he have to arrest Christians? *Priests in the synagogues.*
3. Where was Paul headed to complete his mission? *Damascus.*
4. Who did Paul meet on the way to Damascus? *God.*
5. What did God ask Paul? *"Why are you persecuting me?"(Acts 9:4)*
6. What did God do to Paul? *Blinded him for three days.*
7. Who did God send to heal Paul's blindness? *Ananias.*
8. How did Ananias react when he was told to heal Paul? *At first he questioned it, but then he obeyed God.*
9. What changed with Paul after he had his sight back? *He followed God. He preached the gospel wherever he went.*
10. Did people believe Paul was changed? *Not at first, but he was so different, they realized something had changed him.*

Go Further

1. When Paul met God, he was changed. When someone chooses to follow God, what kind of change happens to them? (See 2 Corinthians 5:17.) *They become a new person.*
2. What does someone do to become a member of God's family? (See Romans 10:9.) *Openly declare that Jesus is Lord and believe that he rose from the day.*
3. How can you share your faith with others?

Wrap It Up!

Refer to the time line.

At first, Paul did not believe that Jesus was the Messiah. He was determined to wipe out Jesus' followers. After God spoke to him loud and clear, Paul changed. He went from being a persecutor of Christians to a preacher of Christ. Paul spread the Gospel not only to the Jews, but also to the non-Jews. The non-Jews were called *Gentiles*. Just as Paul was changed after he began following God, we change when we become children of God. We put away our old selves and become imitators of Christ, telling everyone about the God we serve!

LESSON OVERVIEW

Children will learn what brought about the Council of Jerusalem and its effects. Namely, that through grace, God offers salvation to all people.

Acts 15

Council of Jerusalem

Introduce It!

Time Line

50 A.D.

Key Events & People

Meeting of the Council of Jerusalem; Barnabas, Paul, Peter, Pharisees

Time Line Materials needed. (See p. 4.)

Begin the lesson by praying for each child individually. Thank God for each of them.

Memory Verse

For God saved us and called us to live a holy life. He did this, not because we deserved it, but because that was his plan.

2 Timothy 1:9

After Jesus' death and resurrections in 30 A.D., people had a lot of questions. Some believed that he was the Messiah. Others believed he was not. Paul originally persecuted Christians, but God spoke to him, and then he believed. Refer to the time line 38 A.D. Paul spread the gospel wherever he went. He spoke to Jews and non-Jews about Jesus. Remember that God's people were the Jews. They were Abraham's descendants. But when Jesus came, he preached a message that was for the whole world.

Place time line marker at 50 A.D.

The new believers, called *Gentiles*, did not know the Jewish rules. Some of the Jewish people were causing a fuss because of the new group of believers.

Tell It!

Choose a way to tell the story while reading the account from the Bible or telling it in your own words. Ideas for creative storytelling include acting it out, using props, or incorporating pictures.

Jews vs. Gentiles

In 50 A.D., the Jews and the Gentiles were not getting along. A group of Jewish leaders, the Pharisees, thought only Jews could be saved by faith in Jesus. They did not like Gentiles, who were unclean in their eyes. Big problems were happening between the two groups.

Start the lesson with the On Your Line activity on page 196.

ON YOUR LINE

So, what is the difference between Jewish and Gentile members of God's family?

There really weren't a lot of differences between Jewish and Gentile believers. The Jews followed the Old Testament Laws, but both groups believed in Jesus. The Pharisees felt that Jesus's gift of salvation from what he did on the cross was only available to Jews who followed Old Testament law.

Jew	Jew and Gentile	Gentile
Descendant of Abraham	Can believe Jesus is the Messiah	Not a descendant of Abraham
God's chosen people	Can believe in Jesus' Resurrection	
Follow Old Testament law	Can have the Holy Spirit	

Council of Jerusalem

Because no one was sure what was true, Paul and his friend Barnabas went to Jerusalem for an important meeting. They wanted to talk to the apostles, Jesus' closest friends, to hear their opinion on how to be saved. This meeting was called the Council of Jerusalem, and it was held in 50 A.D. Refer to the time line.

Paul and Barnabas were welcomed by the whole church when they arrived. Let's pretend we are welcoming Paul and Barnabas. Children clap their hands.

This meeting lasted for a long time. At one point, Peter stood up and shared his opinion. He said, "Listen everyone, I've preached to Jews and Gentiles. God gave the Holy Spirit to both groups. He loves everyone. He knows everyone's hearts. So why are we arguing about this? Why are we giving the new Gentile believers so many rules? They believe the same things that we do. Jesus saved them from their sins the same way he saved us. We did not deserve to be saved, but he saved us anyway" (See Acts 15:7–11.)

After Peter spoke, the council agreed that he was right. Let's celebrate! Clap your hands with me. Children clap their hands. Jesus died for everyone. As a result, the Gentiles did not have to follow the Old Testament law.

Then the council sent messengers to the churches. Stop giving the Gentiles so many rules, they said! Jews and Gentiles can worship together!

Pray It!

Dear God, thank you for sending your Son to save ALL people. It doesn't matter if we are Jew or Gentile, big or small, old or young, sick or healthy. You came to save all of us because you love us. Teach me to love others the same way you love me. In Jesus' name, amen.

Apply It!

Choose any of these activities for your lesson. Use more than one if time allows. For any of these activities, discuss the **Talk about It!** questions on page 199 as time allows.

Show It!

Materials
masking tape or rope

On Your Line

Overview

Children form groups based on different statements in order to see that though there may be some differences between us, there are many similarities, too.

Preparation

Use masking tape or rope to make a line down the center of the activity area.

Directions

1. Instruct children on the rules: **I'm going to read some statements. For each one, if the statement is true for you, stand on this side of the line.** Indicate side. **If the statement is NOT true for you, stand on the other side.** Indicate other side.
2. Read the following statements one at a time. Children respond as instructed.
   - **I have a dog.**
   - **I don't have a sister.**
   - **I have blue eyes.**
   - **My favorite color is red.**
   - **I like chocolate more than vanilla.**
   - **Spiders scare me.**
   - **I have eaten sushi.**
   - **I have broken a bone.**
   - **My pants are black today.**
   - **Pizza is my favorite food.**
   - **I love brussels sprouts.**
   - **I have never ridden on a roller coaster.**

Conversation

Did everyone have all of the same answers? Children respond. **Being different doesn't make anyone better or worse than anyone else. Were any of you surprised to find out others had some things in common with you?** Children respond.

Act It Out!

Materials
large sheet of paper
markers
sticky notes

On the Cross

Overview

Children lay their names on a cross as a reminder that Jesus died for them.

Preparation

On large sheet of paper, draw a cross similar to the one on this page. Make sure the cross is as large as the sheet. Place in the middle of the floor or a table, or post on a wall or board.

Directions

1. Ask children, **Did Jesus die to save the Jews or the Gentiles? That's right! Jesus died for both Jews and Gentiles—he died for everyone! That means Jesus died for me and for you, and you, and you. Jesus died for all of us.**
2. Children write their names on a sticky note.
3. Call each child by name, one at a time. When you call their name, each child walks up to the cross and sticks their note to the cross.

Conversation

Early on, many people, both Jews and Gentiles, thought that salvation was only for Jews. Nowadays, some people think salvation through Jesus is only for Gentiles and not for Jews! Neither is true. Jesus offers the gift of salvation to ANYONE who believes in him! That includes everyone here on Earth today and anyone who might be here 100 years from now!

Play It!

Jew or Gentile?

> **Materials**
> plastic cups (approximately 100)
> stopwatch or watch with second hand

Overview

Teams race to turn cups either right-side up or right-side down.

Directions

1. Place the cones or cups on the playing area, half of them right-side up and the other right-side down.
2. Divide the children into two teams, the "Jews" and the "Gentiles." Designate one team as owning all the cups that are right-side up. The other team owns the cups that are right-side down.
3. For one minute, children race against the clock and each other to get all of the cones or cups facing their team's way.
4. When time is up, the team with the most cups facing their way answers one of the **Talk about It!** questions on page 199 or recites the memory verse.

Tip

Instead of trying to count all the cups yourself, instruct teams to stack their team's cups. The bigger stack will be the team with the most!

Conversation

Some of the Jewish people in the early days of the church believed Gentiles could not be Christians because they did not follow the Old Testament law. We know from the Council of Jerusalem, and God's Word, that we do not have to follow Jewish law to be saved.

Craft It!

Craft a Card

Materials

colored cardstock or construction paper

crayons or markers

decorative materials (stickers, craft-foam shapes, glitter glue, etc.)

Overview

Children make a card to tell others about Jesus' love.

Directions

1. Each child folds a sheet of cardstock or construction paper in half to form a card.
2. On the inside of the card, children write a message to tell someone that Jesus died on the cross because he loves them.
3. Children use decorative materials to decorate cards.

Conversation

Jesus did not come just to save the Jews. He didn't come to save only the Gentiles. Jesus died on the cross to save EVERYONE!

Snack It!

Council Cookies

Materials

chocolate and vanilla sandwich cookies (2 or 3 per child)

paper plates

Overview

Children enjoy chocolate and vanilla sandwich cookies.

Directions

Children place two or three cookies on a plate and then eat them.

Conversation

Why do you think our cookies have two flavors in one cookies? Children respond. Our cookies today can remind us of what happened at the Council of Jerusalem in 50 A.D. Two sides were different, the Jews and the Gentiles. Our cookies have two different flavors, but they make one good cookie! This reminds us that God's family is made up of lots of different kinds of people. What matters is that God loves everyone, and Jesus died so that anyone who chooses the salvation he offers can become a member of God's family.

Talk about It!

Basic Questions

1. Who did Jesus die for? *Everyone.*
2. Who traveled with Paul to the Council of Jerusalem? *Barnabas.*
3. Which two groups were fighting about salvation through Jesus? *Jews and Gentiles.*
4. What group did Jesus belong to? *Jews.*
5. What set the Jews apart from the Gentiles? *Jews followed Old Testament Law, are descendants of Abraham, and are God's chosen people.*
6. The Pharisees claimed that only who can be saved? *Jews.*
7. Which disciple spoke up at the Council of Jerusalem? *Peter.*
8. Who did Peter say can be saved? *Everyone.*
9. True or false: because we are good people, we are saved. *False. We did nothing to deserve salvation. God gave it to us freely.*
10. What did the Council of Jerusalem decide about the Gentiles and the Old Testament? *Gentiles did not need to follow Old Testament law. They only needed to believe in Jesus.*

Go Further

1. The Council of Jerusalem happened because of an argument. How do you solve arguments?
2. What does a person have to do to be saved?.
3. Acts 15:11 says it is through the grace of Jesus that we are saved. What does that mean? *We cannot do anything to deserve salvation.*

Wrap It Up!

Refer to the time line.

Only two decades after Jesus' death and resurrection, the Council of Jerusalem met to decide who Jesus died for. Paul had been traveling everywhere to spread the news that Jesus is the Messiah. The Pharisees thought Jesus came to save only the Jews, but that was not true. Jesus offers the gift of salvation to all who believe in him!

22

LESSON OVERVIEW

While learning about the first of Paul's missionary journeys, children will begin to understand the dynamic between the Jews and Gentiles at the time. They will also continue learning about the spread of the gospel and the Early Church.

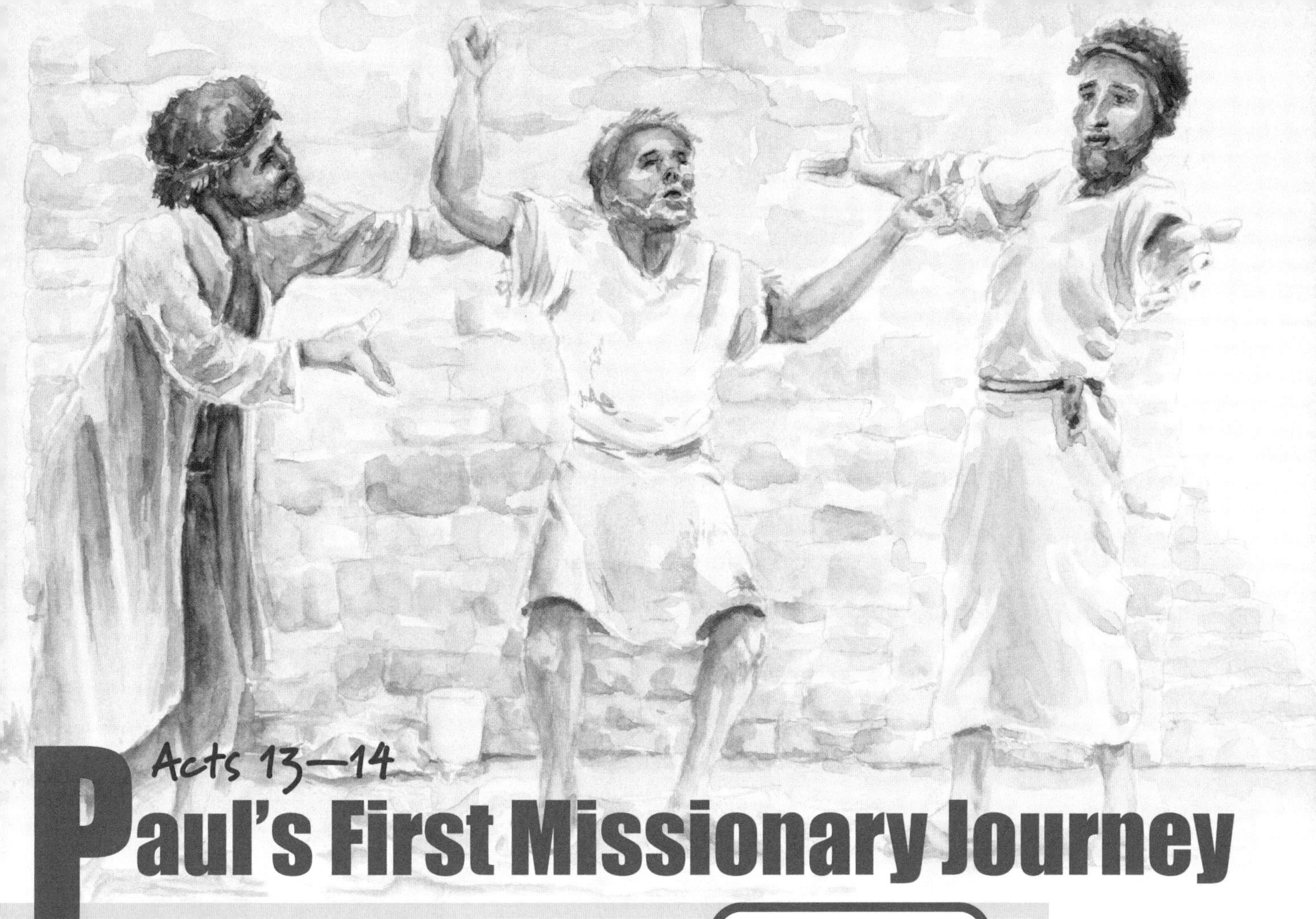

Acts 13—14

Paul's First Missionary Journey

Introduce It!

Time Line

47–49 A.D.

Key Events & People

Paul and Barnabas travel to spread the gospel; Barnabas, John Mark, Paul

A map of the Mediterranean Sea and surrounding lands and Time Line Materials needed. (See p. 4.)

Begin the lesson in prayer. Take time to pray for the people in your life who still need to hear the message of the gospel.

Memory Verse

For I am not ashamed of this Good news about Christ. It is the power of God at work, saving everyone who believes—the Jew first and also the Gentile.

Romans 1:16

The Church was growing. The disciples, not just the original twelve, were preaching and performing miracles in Jesus' name. Though the gospel was spreading and the Church was growing, some groups did not want the message to spread. At first, Paul did not want the message to spread either. Do you remember what he did? Children respond. He had a mission to arrest, imprison, and kill Christians.

Refer to the time line at 38 A.D. After Paul encountered God on the road to Damascus, he began preaching the message of Jesus. Paul eventually became one of the greatest missionaries of the gospel. Place time line marker on 47 A.D. His journey began around 47 A.D. in Antioch. Paul and Barnabas embarked on their first journey to tell the world about Jesus.

Tell It!

Choose a way to tell the story while reading the account from the Bible or telling it in your own words. Ideas for creative storytelling include acting it out, using props, or incorporating pictures.

Note: This story chronologically takes place before the Council of Jerusalem (see p. 192), but the cultural context explained in that lesson is necessary for this lesson.

If you are building a time line with the coloring pages (in back of this book), Paul's First Missionary Journey should come before the Council of Jerusalem.

Paul's Journey

Despite the best attempts of the Jews and the high officials to stop the spread of the gospel and the message of Jesus Christ, it was still spreading! God had a special task for Paul and Barnabas.

Read Acts 13:2.

The Holy Spirit called Paul and Barnabas to deliver God's Word to the people. Along with John Mark, the three set off on the first of Paul's missionary journeys. They were headed to Salamis on the Island of Cyprus.

MAP IT! Refer to a map of the Mediterranean Sea and the surrounding land and islands.

After preaching in Salamis, the three walked to Paphos (still part of the Island of Cyprus), where they met with the governor and a sorcerer. The governor wanted to hear the Word of God and sent for the men. But the sorcerer tried to turn the governor against God. Paul spoke harshly to the sorcerer. He told him to stop confusing people about the truth. The sorcerer became blind, and when the governor saw what happened, he became a believer.

Jealousy Against Paul

After Paphos, Paul and Barnabas started sailing to Perga. There, John Mark left them, heading toward Jerusalem. Paul and Barnabas kept sailing until they reached Antioch in Pisidia. This is not the same Antioch where they began their journey.

Paul and Barnabas spoke boldly about God, and they made some enemies because of it.

Read Acts 13:45.

Large crowds gathered to hear Paul preach. The Jews were jealous. They began saying bad things about Paul and Barnabas.

How would you react if people were saying bad things about you? Children respond. It might make you want to stop doing what you were doing. Do you think Paul and Barnabas stopped telling people about God just because some people were being mean to them? Children respond. No way! They continued preaching the Word of God, so much so that they were kicked out of Antioch!

The Journey Continues

Do you think this was the end of the trip? Children respond. No way! Paul and Barnabas headed to Iconium, where there were more threats against them. They then fled to Lystra.

In Lystra, Paul used the power of the Holy Spirit to heal a crippled man. Because of the Holy Spirit's power working through Paul and Barnabas, the people thought Paul was the false god Hermes, and they thought Barnabas was another false god, Zeus. The people even tried to offer sacrifices to Paul and Barnabas. Paul and Barnabas were shocked! They were not gods! They were preaching the news of the one true God!

Read Acts 14:14–18.

Things got so bad in Lystra that the people threw rocks at Paul and left him for dead. But Paul did not die. After all of this, do you think Paul ended his journey? Children respond. No way! He continued to spread the gospel.

Encouraging the Believers

When Paul and Barnabas traveled, they did not have Bibles to leave with the new believers. The full Bible had not been written yet! To encourage the new believers, Paul and Barnabas returned. They sailed back home the same way they came to check on the believers. They went back to Lystra, Iconium, Antioch in Pisidia, Perga, and then to Attalia to sail back to where they started from in Antioch. Paul and Barnabas even stopped at the places that had not treated them nicely, and they encouraged them!

Pray It!

Dear God, please show me who to share my faith with. When I feel afraid or judged for being a Christian, please be with me. Remind me that you are never far away. In Jesus' name, amen.

Apply It!

Choose any of these activities for your lesson. Use more than one if time allows. For any of these activities, discuss the **Talk about It!** questions on page 209 as time allows.

Show It!

Pack It Up

Materials

suitcase

objects that would be packed for a trip (toothbrush and other toiletries, pajamas, hairbrush, towel, hat, clothing, computer, camera, stuffed animal, etc.)

Overview

Children will discuss what people might pack for a trip.

Preparation

Before class, pack objects in suitcase.

Directions

1. Show suitcase. **When do people use suitcases? What are some of the things they might pack in a suitcase?** Children respond. As children are naming things that might be packed in a suitcase, open suitcase and pull out items as they are named or show items for children to respond to by naming the object.
2. **Have you ever packed a suitcase? Where did you go on your trip?** Children respond.

Conversation

Were there any special jobs that your parents asked you to do on your trip? *(Pack their own suitcase, water plants before leaving, look for street signs to help navigate, etc.)* **Today's Bible story is about a trip that Paul and Barnabas took. Why did they go on this journey?** *(To tell others about Jesus.)*

Paul and Barnabas weren't going away on vacation! They were on a special mission from Jesus to tell others all about the good news of Jesus' death and resurrection and how people can become members of God's family.

Act It Out!

Paul's Trip

Overview

Children have a relay race, pretending to go to the different cities Paul visited.

Materials

masking tape

sheets of paper

marker

Preparation

1. Use masking tape to make a start line on one side of the playing area.
2. On separate sheets of paper, print the following place names: Salamis, Paphos, Perga, Antioch in Pisidia, Iconium, Lystra, Derbe.
3. Arrange the signs you prepared around the room.

Directions

1. **You will follow the journey that Paul and Barnabas took. First you will go to Salamis, then Paphos, Perga, Antioch, Iconium, Lystra, Derbe, and back again.**

1. Children form evenly numbered teams and line up behind the start line.
2. Call out the first city name. **Salamis!** The first player on each team races to touch the Salamis paper.
3. Call out the other city names in order so the players race to touch each paper in order.
4. After touching the Derbe paper, players race back to their team and tag the next players to repeat the action.
5. Continue until every player has had a turn. The first team to finish answers one of the **Talk about It!** questions on page 209.

Tip

Try mixing up the signs and teams between rounds.

Conversation

Everywhere that Paul and Barnabas went on their three-year journey, they boldly shared the Word of God!

Play It!

I'm Going on a Trip

Overview

Children play a travel game.

Directions

1. Children stand or sit in a circle. Depending on the size of your group, age of your children, or the time available, you may need to divide into two or more individual circles.
2. Choose a volunteer to begin the game. Volunteer says, "I'm going on a trip and I'm taking a . . ." Volunteer then names an item they wish to take on the trip.
3. The player to the right of the volunteer names the item named before and then adds an item of their own choosing.
4. The next player and all remaining players must name each item previously mentioned, in order, before adding an item of their own choosing.
5. If a player makes a mistake, they answer, or choose a volunteer to answer, one of the **Talk about It!** questions on page 209.

Conversation

Who remembers how long Paul and Barnabas were on this trip? Children respond. **Three years! Three years of traveling by sea and preaching the Word of God! Do you think Paul and Barnabas would have needed any of the items we listed?** Children respond.

Craft It!

Cross Necklaces

Overview

Children make two necklaces: one for themselves and one to give to someone else.

Materials

plastic cording
scissors
masking tape
pony beads
cross-shaped beads
super glue or clear nail polish

Directions

1. Children cut two lengths of cording, each approximately 36-inches long.
2. Children fold a piece of masking tape over one end of each cord to stop beads from falling off the cord as they work.
3. Children thread pony beads and cross-shaped beads on the cording until they are pleased with the design.
4. When done beading, children remove the masking-tape stopper and tie a knot at the ends of the cord, so the necklace can be easily pulled on or off over the head.
5. Children secure the knot with a few drops of super glue or clear nail polish.
6. Children repeat to make a second necklace.

Conversation

Why do you think you made two necklaces? Children respond. **Scripture tells us that Paul and Barnabas boldly told people about Christ. We should be doing the same! You will keep one necklace for yourself, but your challenge is to find someone to give the second cross necklace to. When you give it to them, boldly tell them about Jesus. Remember that you don't need to be mean to be bold. Just be excited!**

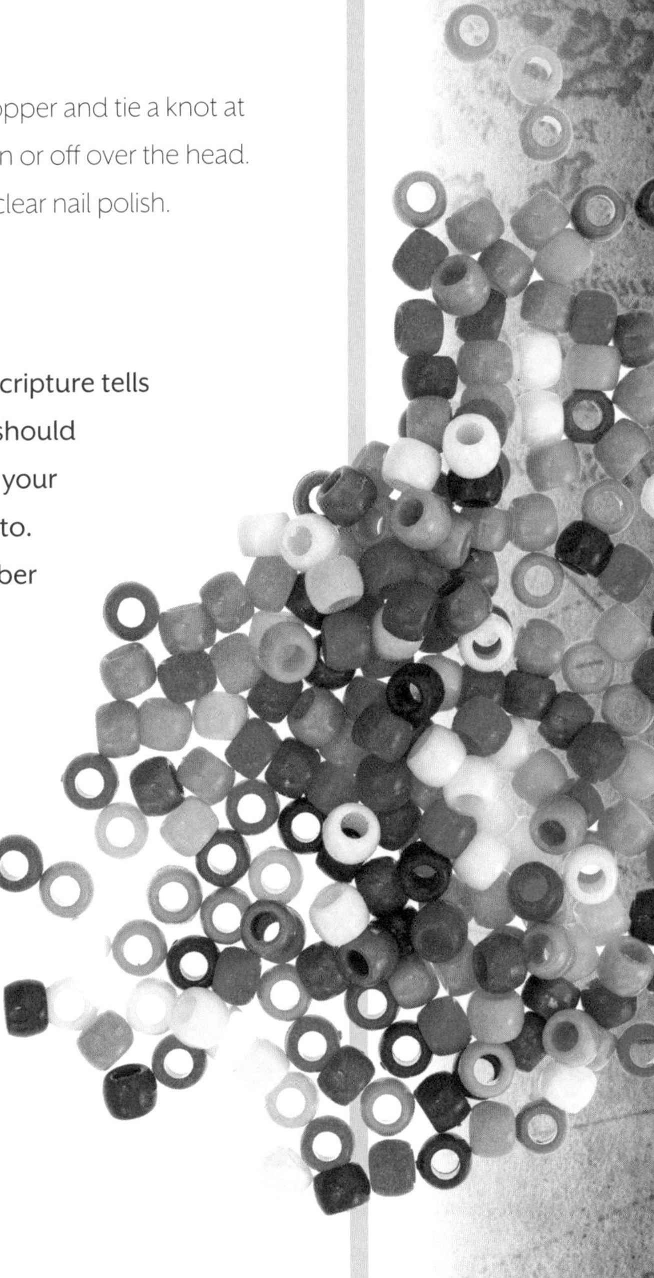

Snack It!

Sailor's Snack

Overview

Children enjoy a snack that reminds them of Paul's first missionary journey.

Materials

fish-shaped crackers or gummy fish

paper plates or cups

Preparation

Place fish-shaped crackers or gummy fish on paper plates or in cups, preparing one for each child.

Directions

Children enjoy their "fishy" snacks while discussing Paul's missionary journey. In addition to the conversation below, be sure to discuss the **Talk about It!** questions on page 209.

Conversation

How did Paul and Barnabas get to the cities they visited? Children respond. By boat! They could not hop on a plane or travel by car. The only way to get to where they were going was to sail!

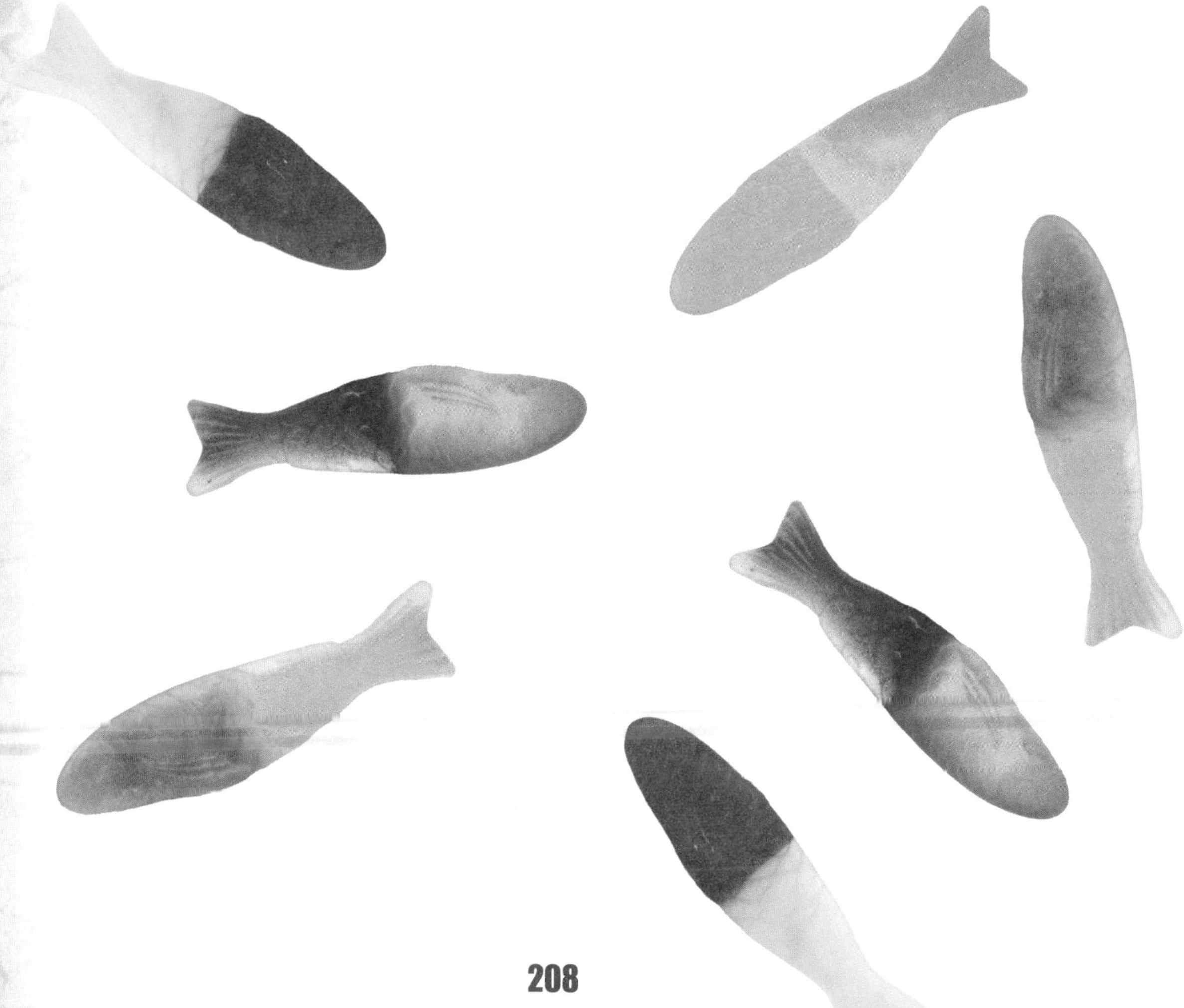

Talk about It!

Basic Questions

1. What two men were called by the Holy Spirit to travel spreading God's Word? *Paul and Barnabas.*
2. What city did they start from? *Antioch.*
3. What disciple traveled with them? *John Mark.*
4. They first sailed to the island of ______. *Cyprus.*
5. In Paphos, there was a ______ that was trying to turn people against God and was blinded as punishment. What was he? *A sorcerer.*
6. What group of people turned against Paul because of their jealousy? *The Jews.*
7. John Mark did not travel with Paul the whole time. Where did he return to? *Jerusalem.*
8. After healing a lame man in Lystra, the people though Paul and Barnabas were what? *The false Greek gods, Zeus and Hermes.*
9. What happened after Paul was stoned and left for dead? *They kept traveling.*
10. What did the men do on their return trip home? *Stopped at the places they had visited and encouraged the believers there.*

Go Further

1. What message was so important that Paul did not even let being stoned and left for dead stop him from sharing? *Jesus died and rose again to save everyone from sin.*
2. Paul traveled the world telling people the message of Christ. Where do you take that message to?
3. Who in your life do you need to share Jesus with?

Wrap It Up!

Paul and Barnabas traveled to a lot of places and ministered to many people during their three-year trip. No matter what happened—jealous crowds, threats against their lives, and even being left for dead—Paul and Barnabas boldly kept spreading the message of Jesus Christ!

23

LESSON OVERVIEW

Through Paul's suffering, children will learn how we are to rejoice always, working for the progress of the gospel no matter what happens.

Acts 27—28

Paul in Rome

Introduce It!

Time Line

61–68 A.D.

Key Events & People

Paul travels to Rome, is shipwrecked, writes letters, and Dies; Paul

Memory Verse

Always be full of joy in the Lord. I say it again—rejoice!

Philippians 4:4

A map of the Mediterranean Sea and surrounding lands and Time Line Materials needed. (See p. 4.)

Begin the lesson in prayer. Thank God for the example Paul set for us through his ability to rejoice in the midst of his suffering.

The year is 61 A.D., (place time line marker on 61 A.D.), and Paul is a prisoner. We read in the book of Acts that Paul was arrested, not because of any crime that he committed, but because he was boldly preaching the message of Jesus Christ. Some of the Jewish leaders did not like Paul preaching the message of Jesus. They felt it threatened Jewish traditions, so they had him arrested. There were even plans to kill him, but because Paul was a Roman citizen, he was kept safe. He had requested a trial with the Roman Emperor, and it was granted. Our lesson begins with Paul on his way to Rome for a trial.

Tell It!

Choose a way to tell the story while reading the account from the Bible or telling it in your own words. Ideas for creative storytelling include acting it out, using props, or incorporating pictures.

The Voyage to Rome

Paul had been in prison for two years in Caesarea. Then it came time for him to travel to Rome for his trial. But it was not an easy trip. The wind was blowing in the wrong direction, which made the ship move very slowly. Winter was approaching, which was a dangerous time to travel. The ship had docked at a port in Fair Havens, but the captain still thought they could make it to Rome. Paul tried to warn him to stay where they were, but he would not listen.

They set sail again and got stuck in a typhoon! The ship rocked violently back and forth. Sailors started throwing cargo overboard to lighten the ship. It rained hard for days, and they ran out of food.

"Why didn't you listen to me?" Paul said to the captain. "I told you we should have stayed where we were safe." Then, Paul looked around at all the scared sailors. "Don't worry, everyone. An angel of the Lord came to me last night. He told me that God will protect everyone on this ship. Even though the ship will go down, not one person will die" (See Acts 27:21–26).

Just as Paul had said, the ship hit shallow water and began to break apart. Everyone was terrified.

Read Acts 27:42–44.

If you were Paul, a prisoner who had just survived a huge storm and shipwreck, how would you feel? Children respond. Things were rough for Paul, but God protected him.

Finally in Rome

Paul's ship had wrecked on the island of Malta. After gathering supplies, the crew got another boat and set sail again for Rome. This time they made it to Rome! Hooray! Remember, Paul was still a prisoner. How do you think he was treated when he arrived in Rome? Children respond.

Read Acts 28:16.

Paul was basically under house arrest. He was not in a prison cell; he was in a house with a soldier guarding him. From 61 A.D. to 63 A.D., Paul was allowed to preach and teach people who came to see him. He also spent time writing during his imprisonment. During those two years, Paul wrote letters to the church of Ephesus, Colossi, Philippi, and to his friend Philemon. Paul called himself a "prisoner of Christ." He was a prisoner, but he still rejoiced. He was furthering the gospel, which was Paul's main goal.

Paul Is Martyred

Paul had a passion for spreading the gospel. He wanted everyone, Jew or Gentile, to become a member of God's family.

Read Acts 21:13.

He wasn't worried about what could happen to him; he only wanted people to know about Jesus.

Paul was released from prison and traveled again to spread the gospel. Again, he was arrested, and this time he was put to death. The Bible doesn't tell us of Paul's death, but it is believed that he was beheaded in 68 A.D. by order of Emperor Nero. His trips telling people about Christ were at an end, but efforts like his to spread the gospel continue to this day.

Pray It!

Dear God, thank you for Paul's example. Thank you for showing us what it means to truly love you. Please give us courage when people ask us about our faith. Help us to boldly declare what we believe. In Jesus' name, amen.

Apply It!

Choose any of these activities for your lesson. Use more than one if time allows. For any of these activities, discuss the **Talk about It!** questions on page 217 as time allows.

Show It!

Materials

clear plastic bottle with lid

water

blue food coloring

mineral oil

duct tape

Ocean in a Bottle

Overview

Children make miniature waves with a bottle filled with blue water and mineral oil.

In today's Bible story, we heard about a terrible storm that sent huge waves crashing into Paul's ship—and eventually wrecked the ship! We're going to look at a bottle that can make waves, but it won't wreck any ships.

Preparation

Before class, fill the plastic bottle halfway with water. Add several drops of blue food coloring to the bottle. Fill bottle the rest of the way with mineral oil. Screw lid on bottle and secure by wrapping duct tape around the bottle and lid.

Note: If you have a large group, you may want to prepare more than one bottle.

Directions

1. Show the bottle. Ask a volunteer to hold the bottle horizontally, and then to gently rock the bottle to make waves.
2. Allow a few minutes for different children to use the wave-making bottle.

Conversation

The waves in this bottle remind us of our Bible story and the waves that crashed into Paul's ship and wrecked it. But the waves can also remind us that Paul was on the ship to tell others about Jesus. And even though bad things sometimes happened to him, Paul always rejoiced in God's great love and praised him. We can praise God, too—in bad times or good times, God always loves us and is deserving of our praise.

Act It Out!

Paul's Shipwreck

Overview

Children use fabric to make waves and act out the story of Paul's shipwreck.

Materials

large cardboard box

one or more lengths of blue fabric (yardage, bed sheets, tablecloths, etc.)

Bible-times costumes or bathrobes (optional)

Directions

1. Select a few volunteers to pretend to be Paul and a few sailors and stand in the large cardboard box in the center of the activity area.
2. Remaining children take the lengths of blue fabric, stretch them out, and then move them up and down to create a wave effect.
3. Briefly retell the Bible story as children act out the action.

Optional

Children pretending to be Paul or sailors wear Bible-times costumes or bathrobes.

Conversation

Imagine being in a shipwreck like the one Paul encountered! God was protecting Paul and keeping him safe. Paul's work was not finished. God needed him in Rome!

Play It!

Guard the Prisoners

Overview

Children play a game where they pretend to be prisoners, a prison guard, or jail breakers.

Directions

Materials

3–5 hula hoops or rope circles

1. Place hula hoops or rope circles on the floor in the playing area.
2. Choose two volunteers. One volunteer will be the Prison Guard, while the other volunteer will be the Jail Breaker. The remaining players become prisoners and stand inside the hula hoops or rope circles.
3. Jail Breaker tries to tag players in the prisons to free them, all while trying not to get tagged by the Prison Guard.
4. Once a prisoner is tagged, that player becomes a Jail Breaker and also tries to free other players.
5. Play continues until leader stops the action or if all the prisoners are free. Repeat game with new volunteers as time and interest allow.

Conversation

Our game had a prison guard just like Paul had a guard in Rome. In Ephesians 3:1, Paul refers to himself as a "prisoner of Christ." What do you think that means? Children respond. **Paul realized that though he was a prisoner, God still had a job for him to do! It was part of God's plan for his life.**

Craft It!

Posters of Paul

Materials
- Bibles
- large sheets of butcher paper
- markers

Overview

Children form teams to create posters about Paul.

Directions

1. Children divide into teams of three or four to create posters advertising Paul's arrival in their city.
2. In addition to drawing a picture of Paul, teams should try to include as many facts about Paul as they can remember.
3. After teams finish, teams share their posters with the rest of the group.

Conversation

What a life Paul lived! He told so many people about Christ, and through God's Word, his influence is still strong today.

Snack It!

Roman Munchies

Materials
- cheese cubes
- grapes
- crackers or cubes of bread
- bowls
- large spoons or tongs
- paper plates

Overview

Children eat foods that Paul and Romans may have eaten.

Preparation

Place each snack item in a separate bowl and place on table.
Place a large spoon or tong next to each bowl for children to use to serve themselves.

Directions

1. Give each child a paper plate.
2. Children use utensils to place chosen snack items on their plate.
3. Children eat their snack while engaged in conversation below and discussing **Talk about It!** questions on page 217.

Conversation

If the people of Paul's day wanted a snack, could they grab a bag of chips or a box of candy? Children respond. No way! There were no stores or junk food. Our snack today reminds us of the life Paul lived in Rome and the type of snacks he might have eaten.

Talk about It!

Basic Questions

1. Why was Paul in prison? *He was arrested for teaching about Jesus Christ.*
2. Where was Paul headed to? *Rome.*
3. Who did Paul want a trial before? *Roman Emperor.*
4. On his way to Rome, what happened to Paul? *There was a storm and shipwreck.*
5. What did the angel of the Lord tell Paul about the storm? *The ship would go down, but everyone would live.*
6. What conditions did Paul live in once in Rome? *Under house arrest with a guard.*
7. What did Paul do while living in Rome? *Preached and wrote letters.*
8. How long was Paul a prisoner in Rome? *Two years.*
9. Through all of the bad things that happened to Paul, what did he do? *Rejoice.*
10. The Bible doesn't tell us how Paul died, but what does tradition say happened? *He was beheaded.*

Go Further

1. Read Philippians 4:4. What does Paul say to always do? *Always be full of joy in the Lord.*
2. Think of all of the bad stuff that happened to Paul. How could he still be rejoicing when so much bad had happened? *He trusted God.*
3. How can we, like Paul, rejoice always?

Wrap It Up!

Refer to the time line at 68 A.D.

Paul died for his faith. He was a very important person to the Early Church. He traveled the world with the goal of telling everyone, Jew and Gentile, about Jesus. Things were not always smooth sailing in Paul's life. No matter what happened to him, Paul lived joyfully for the Lord, pressing on toward the goal.

24

LESSON OVERVIEW

Studying the final book of the Bible, children will learn what God says eternity will look like.

Revelation 21; 22:1–6

The Book of Revelation

Introduce It!

Time Line

90–96 or 68–69 A.D.

Key Events & People

Eternity; God, John

Memory Verse

"I am the Alpha and the Omega—the beginning and the end," says the Lord God. "I am the one who is, who always was, and who is still to come—the Almighty One."

Revelation 1:8

Time Line Materials needed. (See p. 4.)

Begin the lesson in prayer. Thank God that he has always been and will always be!

Today's lesson is kind of a mystery. We know that around 90–96 or 68–69 A.D., the apostle John wrote the book of Revelation. Place time line marker on time line. Revelation means to reveal something. Say that you are playing Hide-and-Seek and you find someone's hiding spot. You have revealed where they are hiding.

This last book of the Bible was revealed to John by God. It reveals the things yet to come. The Book of Revelation tells us what eternity will be like, but we don't know when eternity will take place. We do know that it is the forever home for all who believe in Christ Jesus.

Tell It!

Choose a way to tell the story while reading the account from the Bible or telling it in your own words. Ideas for creative storytelling include acting it out, using props, or incorporating pictures.

What Is Heaven Like?

Read 1 Corinthians 2:9.

Scripture tells us that Heaven is going to be so amazing that we can't even imagine it! There is a lot we do not know about Heaven, but Scripture does tell us some things about it.

What do you think Heaven will look and be like? Children respond.

If we want to know what Heaven will be like, where should we go to find out? Should we ask a friend, or look it up online? Children respond. No! The only place we can learn about Heaven is from God, in the Bible.

Let's discover what God tells us Heaven is like by looking up some verses in the book of Revelation. After we read each verse, draw a small picture or symbol that reminds you what that verse told you.

Give each child a piece of paper and a crayon or marker.

Read Revelation 21:4.

In Heaven, there will be no crying, no death, and no pain. Draw a picture on your paper to help you remember that.

The next verses I'll read tell us about the New Jerusalem. As I read, draw a picture on your paper of what you think the New Jerusalem will look like.

Read Revelation 21:10–21.

Revelation tells us what the city will look like: streets of gold, pearly gates, and jewels all over.

Read Revelation 21:23.

This verse tells us about something that is NOT in Heaven. What is not there? Children respond. There is no sun or moon in Heaven! The light in Heaven comes from God himself. Draw a picture to remind you that there is no moon or sun in Heaven.

Read Revelation 22:1–6.

Draw a picture of the tree of life that Scripture tells us will be in Heaven.

Who Goes to Heaven?

Revelation chapters 21–22 give us some snippets of what Heaven might look like. While we know some of what it might look like, how do we know who will be in Heaven? Again, we need to go straight to the source of authority, God's Word.

Read Revelation 21:3.

We know that God will be in Heaven and that he is there now. But who gets to go to Heaven? Let's look at two passages to help us answer this question.

Read Revelation 7:9 and 21:27.

Heaven will be full of people from every tribe, language, and nation. Heaven is full of people from all different walks of life, but Revelation 21:27 tells us about the one thing that all of these people have in common. They are all written in the Lamb's Book of Life. That means, in order to go to Heaven, you must be a child of God, a Christian! Heaven is for Christians only. It is the eternal home for believers!

Pray It!

Dear God, thank you for preparing a place for us after death. Thank you for assuring us that you will take care of us always. Remind me that I don't have to fear death because I believe in you. Help me to share my faith with others so they can go to Heaven with me. In Jesus' name, amen.

Apply It!

Choose any of these activities for your lesson. Use more than one if time allows. For any of these activities, discuss the **Talk about It!** questions on page 225 as time allows.

Show It!

Mobius Magic

Materials

two strips of paper, approximately 2x12-inches in size

tape

scissors

Overview

Children experiment with a Mobius strip and discuss what has no beginning or end.

Eternity has no beginning or end. This is a tough concept to wrap your brain around! Let's look at something else that apparently has no beginning or end.

Directions

1. Hold up two strips of paper. **I need a volunteer to come here and show me where each of these strips begins and ends.** Select a volunteer to complete the action.
2. Tape one end from each of the two strips together, making sure tape covers the join completely.
3. Before joining the remaining two ends together, flip one end over. Then tape, again making sure the tape completely covers the join. **Now we have what is called a Mobius strip.** Ask a volunteer to tell you where the strip begins and ends. **There is no beginning or end!**
4. Use the scissors to cut a slit in the middle of the strip, parallel to the edges. Cut down the center of the strip.
5. Open loop to show that it is still in one piece but bigger than before. If you have time and are able to do so, cut the strip in half again.

Small Group Option

Give each child a pair of strips. Instruct them step-by-step to complete the directions given above.

Conversation

This Mobius strip reminds us of eternity because it has no beginning or end but just keeps growing bigger. This is like God's love because it, too, has no beginning or end, and just grows bigger and bigger!

Act It Out!

Praise Party

Materials

children's worship music and player

party supplies (decorations, hats, noise makers, rhythm instruments, poppers, balloons, confetti, etc.)

Overview

Children have a party to celebrate eternal life.

Directions

Play children's worship music as children use party supplies to enjoy a Praise Party.

Conversation

In Heaven, we will be with God, praising him for all eternity. Do we have to wait until we get to Heaven to praise God? No way! We can and should praise him every day!

Play It!

Everybody's "It!"

Overview

Children play a version of Tag.

Directions

In this game of tag, everyone is "It." If anyone tags you, you are out of the game, because everyone is "It."

Conversation

In our game, who was "It?" Everyone was! This game can remind us of Heaven. Not because we'll be playing games of Tag forever and ever. But because of who can go to Heaven. Who can go to Heaven? Children respond.

People from every tribe, language, and nation will be in Heaven. The only requirement to get into Heaven is that you must be a believer in Jesus, a member of God's family.

Craft It!

Scroll Wall Art

Materials

Light brown or beige paper

crayons or markers

10-inch long thin dowels (2 per child)

glue

30-inch length of cord or yarn (1 per child)

Overview

Children make a scroll-inspired picture of Heaven.

Directions

1. Children take a sheet of paper, crumple it up, then smooth it out, and draw what they think Heaven might look like. If any children don't want to draw pictures, they can copy the words of the verse, Revelation 1:8, from a Bible.
2. Children center a dowel at the top of the page, glue it in place, and then roll the dowel in the paper for one or two turns. Children place a few dots of glue to hold dowel in place. Repeat at bottom of page.
3. Tie each end of the cord or yarn to either end of the top dowel. Set aside to dry.

Conversation

When John wrote the book of Revelation, he wrote on a scroll. Hang your scroll art in your bedroom to remind you about Revelation and Heaven. No one knows exactly what Heaven will look like, but the Bible tells us everyone who is a member of God's family will live together in Heaven forever!

Snack It!

Eternity Donuts

Materials

donuts, any flavors (regular or miniature, but they should have holes)

paper plates

Optional: the sprinkles on sprinkled donuts can represent the jewels mentioned in Heaven.

Overview

Children enjoy a donut snack because donuts are circles that don't have a beginning or end—just like eternity.

Directions

1. Children choose a donut and place it on a paper plate.
2. Children eat their donuts while engaging in the conversation below and discussing the **Talk about It!** questions on page 225.

Conversation

Can anyone tell me where their donut begins and ends? Children respond. You can't. It's a circle, so it doesn't have a beginning or an ending. What else do we know that also has no end? Children respond. Heaven has no end! Scripture tells us that all who believe in the name of Jesus will receive the gift of ETERNAL life—forever with Jesus!

Talk about It!

Basic Questions

1. Heaven is a real place. *True.*
2. Only people from America will be in Heaven. *False; The Bible says people from every tribe and nation will be in Heaven.*
3. There is no crying in Heaven. *True.*
4. You can die in Heaven. *False; The Bible tells us everyone in Heaven will live forever.*
5. You can get sick in Heaven. *False; The Bible tells us that there is no sickness in Heaven.*
6. Light in Heaven comes from God, not the sun. *True.*
7. Your name must be written in the Lamb's Book of Life to be in Heaven. *True.*
8. God will be with us in Heaven for all eternity. *True.*
9. Heaven will not last forever. *False; the Bible tells us Heaven will be our home with God forever.*

Go Further

1. Where does Satan go for all eternity? Read Revelation 20:10. *A fiery lake of burning sulfur.*
2. What happens to those who do not believe in Christ, to those who are not Christians and written in the Lamb's Book of Life? *They do not enter Heaven.*

Wrap It Up!

Heaven is a very real place. All those who are members of God's family get to spend eternity with God. Heaven is the free gift of God's grace, but it is a gift that you must choose to accept.

Revelation 4:8 says, "Holy, holy, holy is the Lord God, the Almighty—the one who always was, who is, and who is still to come." Even those who chose not to accept that Jesus is Lord while on Earth will believe in eternity. Jesus is Lord, now and forever!

25

LESSON OVERVIEW

Children learn that God has always existed, even before the creation of time.

Genesis 1:1

Before Creation

Introduce It!

Time Line
Before Time

Key Events & People
God, Jesus, Holy Spirit

Time Line Materials needed. (See p. 4.)

Begin the lesson in prayer. Thank God that he always has been and always will be.

Today, we'll talk about the beginning of history. Even before creation. To learn about the beginning of history, we have to start before history began. Place time line marker before 4000 B.C. (off of the time line). **Genesis 1:1-2 tells us that the earth was formless and empty. There were no trees, rivers, stars, animals, humans—nothing. There was only God. God existed before anything else.**

Memory Verse

Before the mountains were born, before you gave birth to the earth and the world, from beginning to the end, you are God.

Psalm 90:2

Tell It!

Choose a way to tell the story while reading the account from the Bible or telling it in your own words. Ideas for creative storytelling include acting it out, using props, or incorporating pictures.

Did anyone notice that we put our time line marker off of the actual time line? Does anyone have a guess as to why we did that? Children respond. **We placed our time line marker before the time line because God has always been. Before the creation of our world, God was.**

Read Genesis 1:1.

The very first words of the Bible tell us that God was there before the beginning. Before our world, before our universe was even created, God was already there. Do you think God was by himself? Children respond. **No way!**

God exists in three persons—the Father, the Son, and the Holy Spirit. This is called the *Trinity*. There are three persons, but only one God. All three persons of the Trinity were present before the beginning of the world. But since I wasn't there, you shouldn't take my word for it. Let's read what God, who was there before creation, has to say about it in his Word.

Read Psalm 90:2.

God is eternal. That means that he always has been and always will be. God has no beginning, and he has no end. There was never a time when God hasn't been around. He was never born. He has no birthday. Take time to explain how Christmas is the celebration of Jesus' earthly birthday.

Pray It!

**Dear God, thank you for creating me.
Thank you for thinking that I am so important that you would create me along with everything else you created. In Jesus' name, amen.**

Apply It!

Choose any of these activities for your lesson. Use more than one if time allows. For any of these activities, discuss the **Talk about It!** questions on page 232 as time allows.

Show It

Infinity Sign

Overview

Children explore an infinity sign and discuss eternity, which also has no beginning or end.

Materials
papers with an infinity sign drawn on them

Directions

Select a few children to come up and identify the starting point of each infinity sign.

Conversation

You all did a great job trying to find the start of the infinity signs, but you just can't. Unlike a line, an infinity sign goes on and on. They don't have starting or ending points. These symbols can remind us of God. He doesn't have a beginning or an ending point either—God is eternal.

Act It Out!

Birthday Statues

Overview

Children take the form of statues of people at a various ages.

Directions

1. Children divide into two teams.
2. On their team's turn, each team member picks an age—from zero to 100—and thinks about how someone that age might act on their birthday.
3. On your signal, the teams freeze in position like someone of the age they were thinking. The other team tries to guess how old each person is acting.
4. If a guess is correct, that person unfreezes.
5. When everyone on the team has been unfrozen, the other team has a turn.
6. Continue playing as time and interest allow.

Conversation

You all did a great job acting like birthday boys and girls of all ages! Birthdays are so fun! There are cakes and presents and friends! A birthday can be one of the best days of the year! If time allows, select a few volunteers to share about their favorite birthday.

As fun as birthdays are, how would you feel if you did not have a birthday? Since our birthdays celebrate the day that we were born, God doesn't have a birthday! He was never born! He is eternal, so he doesn't have a birthday.

Even though God doesn't have a birthday, we can celebrate that he is eternal and will always be with us! He never had a beginning, so that means he will never have an end either! That's something worth celebrating.

Optional

If time allows, throw a "God Is Eternal Celebration," (like a birthday party), celebrating that he will always be with us!

Play It!

Line Up by . . .

Overview

Children line up in order of categories.

Directions

Call out a category as children race to line up in order. If needed, kids divide into smaller groups.

- Tallest to shortest
- Alphabetical (first name)
- Clothing color (rainbow order)
- Oldest to youngest
- Birth month

Conversation

Have kids try to figure out where God's birthday would fall in the lineup.

You might be thinking that God's birthday would be in December (Christmas), but God does not have a birthday! He is eternal. He has no beginning and no end. He always has been, so he has no birthday!

Craft It!

Eternity Bracelet

Materials

craft cord in various colors

scissors

washers (1 per child)

Overview

Kids will create an eternity bracelet using craft cord and a washer.

Preparation

Cut the craft cord into 6- to 7-inch lengths, preparing two for each child.

Directions

1. Children select a washer and two lengths of craft cord. The cords may be the same color or different colors.
2. Children fold a length of cord in half, place the loop through the washer, and then pull the ends of the cord through the loop, forming a Lark's Head knot (see image). You may wish to demonstrate by making your own bracelet.
3. Children repeat with second length of cord on other side of the washer.
4. Knot the bracelets onto each child's wrist.

Conversation

Our eternity bracelets remind of us of God. The circle washer on our bracelet has no beginning and no end, and neither does God!

Snack It!

Circle Snacks

Materials

circle shaped snacks (cookies, apple rings, circular cereal, etc.);

paper plates

Overview

Children eat circle snacks as a reminder of God's eternity.

Preparation

Place each snack on a separate plate and place on table.

Directions

Children select circle-shaped snacks (cookies, apple rings, circular cereal, etc.), place them on a plate, and then eat their snacks.

Conversation

Our snack today is circular. Because circles have no beginning and no end, they can remind us of God. He is eternal, with no beginning and no end!

Talk about It!

Basic Questions

1. When did creation happen? *About 6000 years ago.*
2. Who did the creating? *God.*
3. Who was there before the creation of our world? *God the Father, God the Son, God the Holy Spirit.*
4. What are the three persons of God called? *The Trinity.*
5. How many Gods are there? *There is one God.*
6. What attribute of God means that he always has been and always will be? *He is eternal.*
7. If God doesn't have a birthday, then what is Christmas? *Christmas is a time to remember Jesus' earthly birthday.*
8. How long has God existed? *Forever! And he will always exist.*
9. What are some names for God? *Creator, Redeemer, Alpha and Omega, Prince of Peace, Healer, Deliver, Savior, Messiah, etc.*

Go Further

1. All three persons of the Trinity were present at creation. Read John 1:1 and Genesis 1:1. Who does each verse talk about being present at creation, before time began?
2. How does it make you feel knowing that God will never end?
3. What are your favorite names for God?

Wrap It Up!

Refer to the time line.

God's Word tells us that before the world was created, before time began, God was there! He is eternal. From our memory verse today, we also know that long after time ends, God will still be there! What a great feeling, knowing that God will always be!

1240–1200 B.C. | Deborah Encourages

1137 B.C. | Gideon Trusts God

1060–1020 B.C. | Samuel Listens

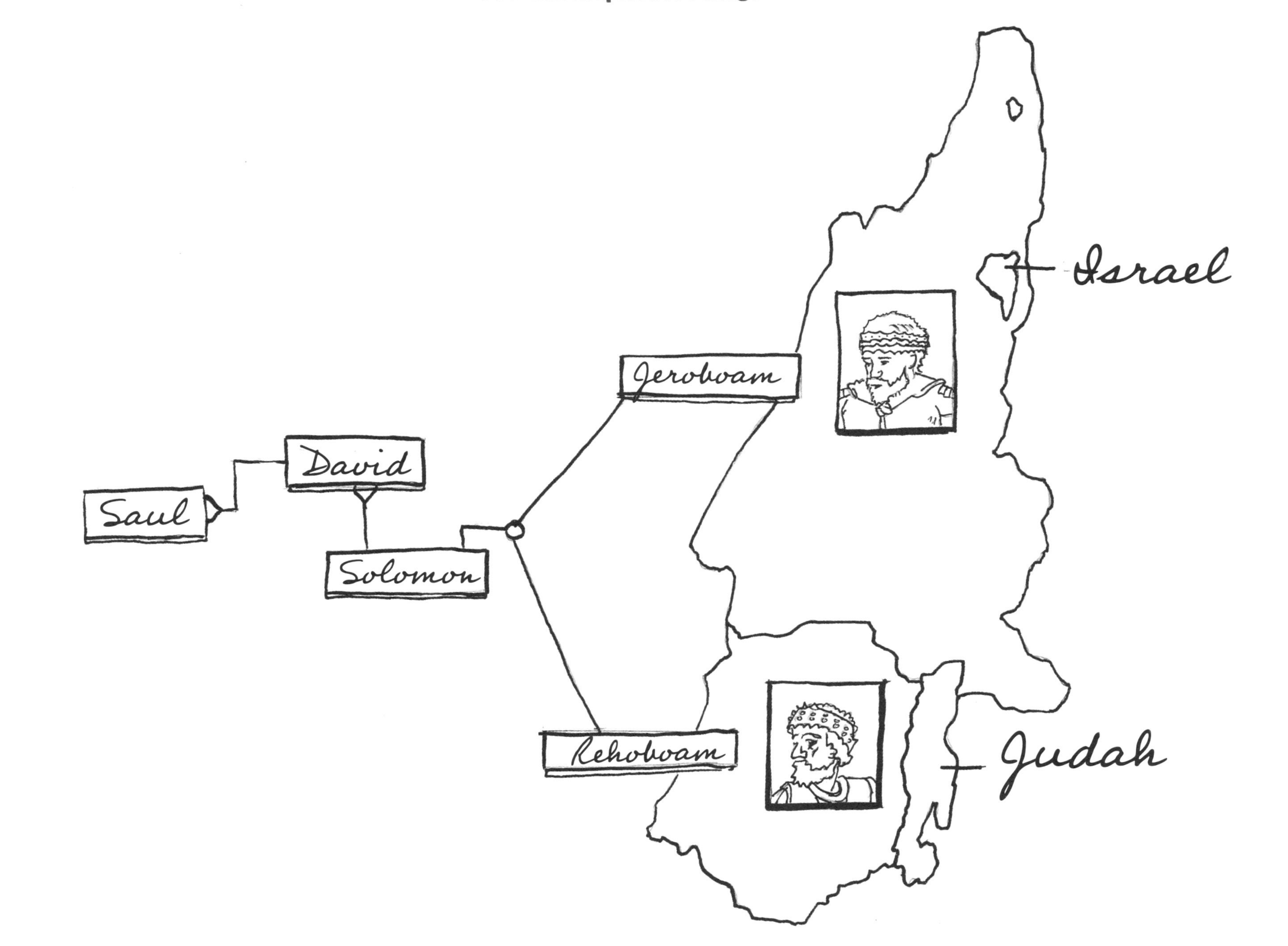
Saul
David
Solomon
Jeroboam
Rehoboam
Israel
Judah

870–845 B.C. | Elijah on Mount Carmel

781 B.C. | Jonah

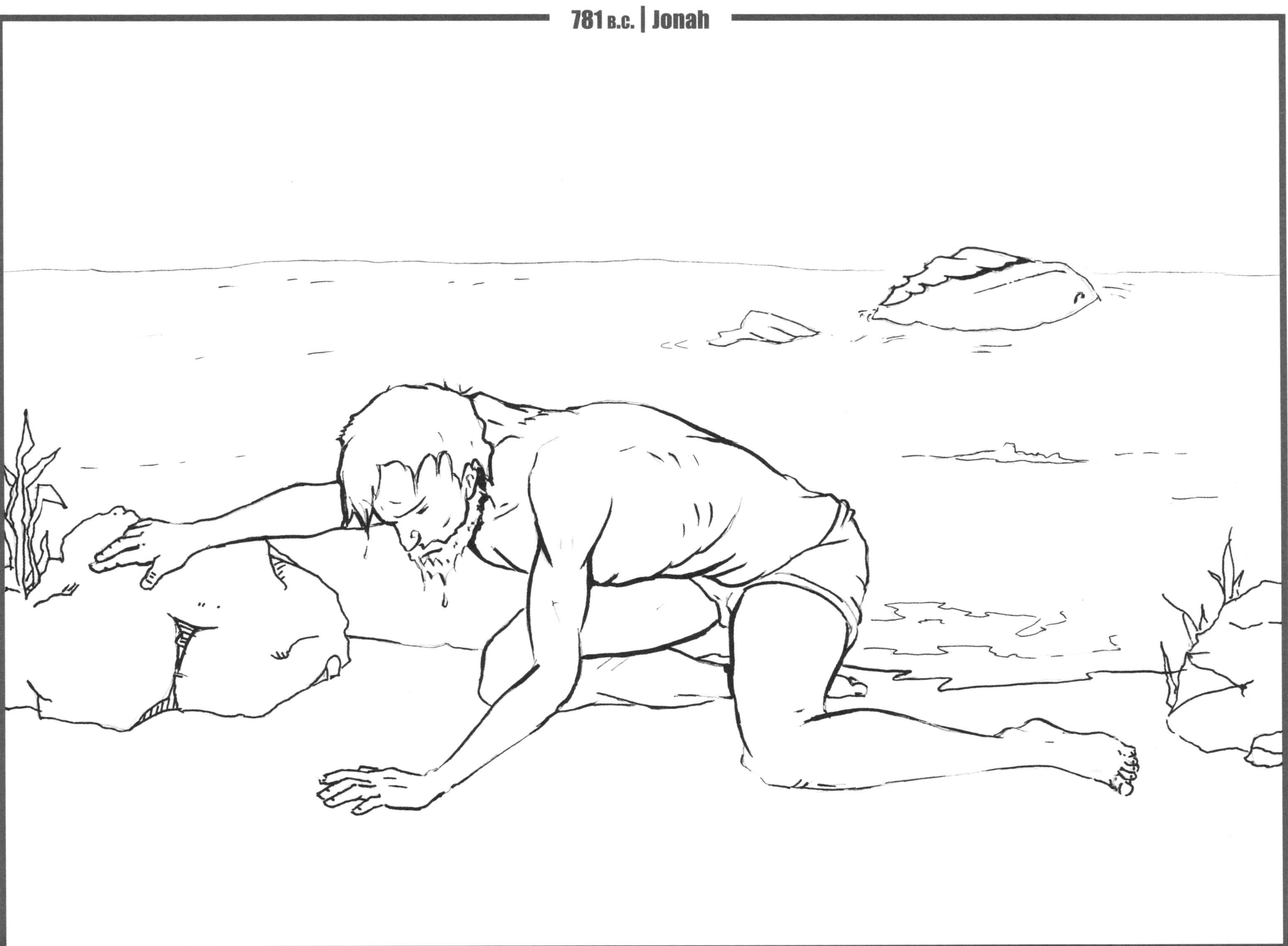

586 B.C. | Jerusalem Destroyed

400 B.C. | Years between Testaments

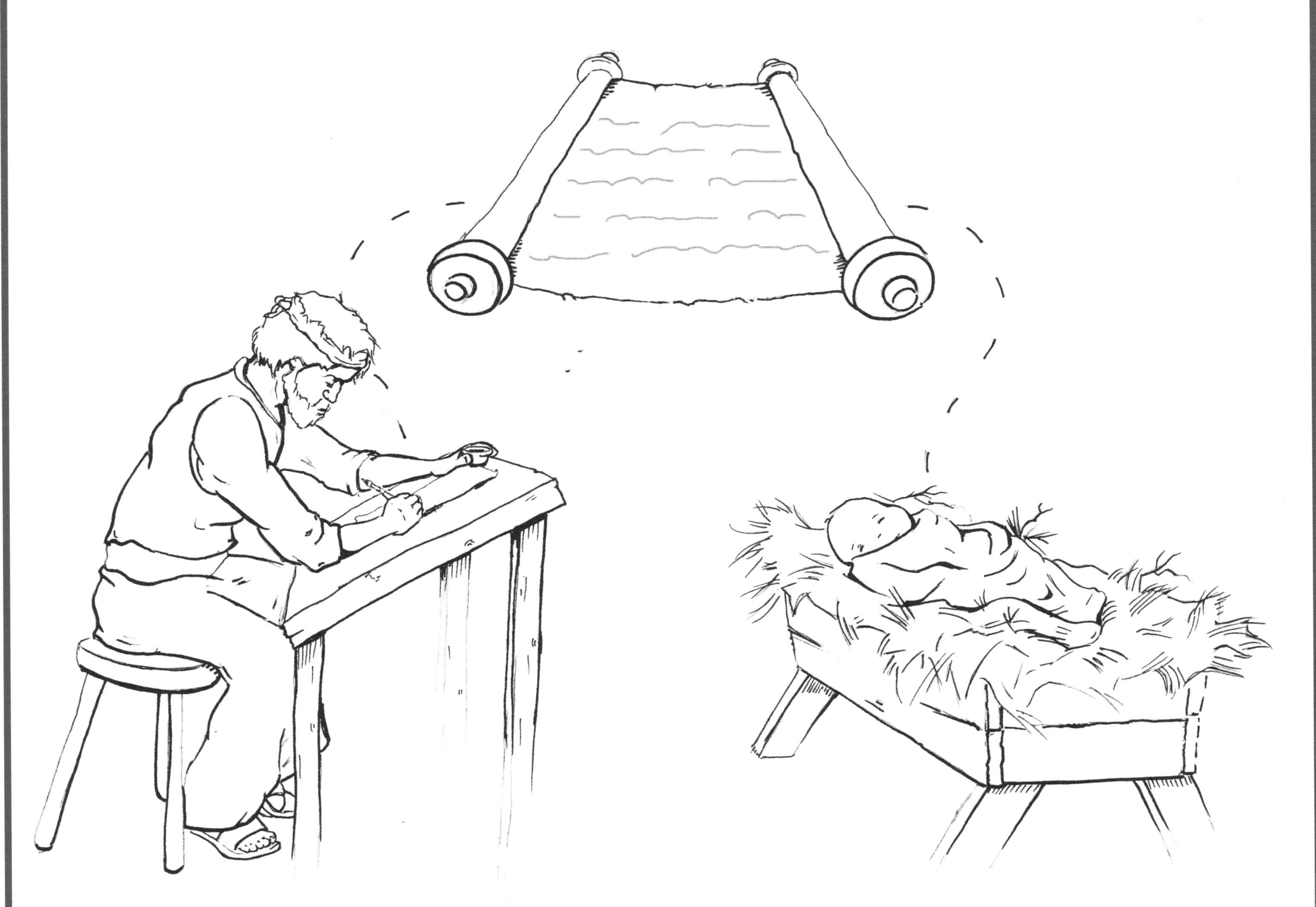

7–5 B.C. | John the Baptist

6–4 B.C. | Jesus' Birth

26 A.D. | Jesus' Baptism

38 A.D. | Paul's Conversion

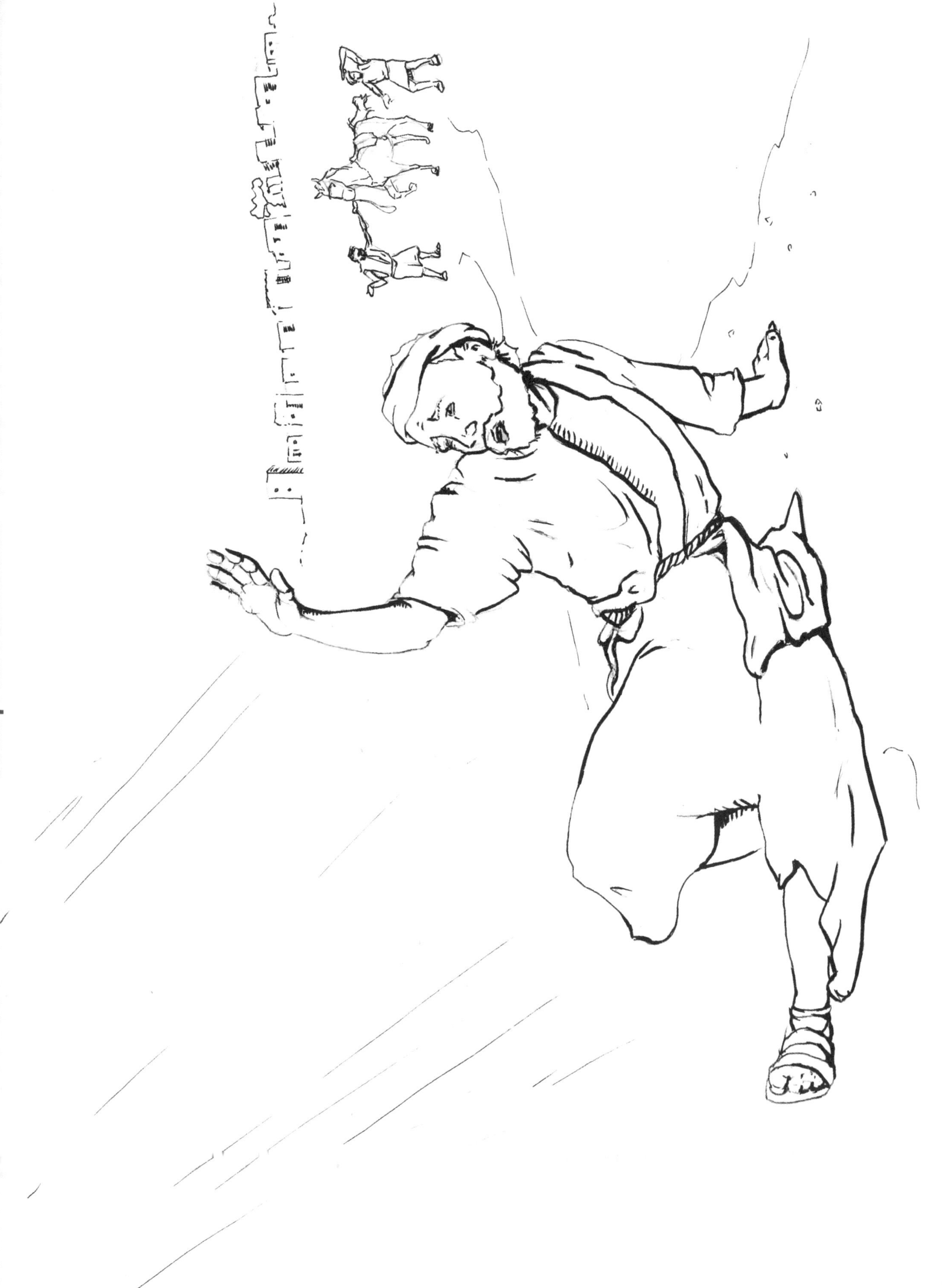

50 A.D. | Council of Jerusalem

47–50 A.D. | Paul's First Missionary Journey

61–68 A.D. | Paul in Rome

90–96 or 68–69 A.D. | The Book of Revelation